Decorative
Cross-Stitch Borders

Sterling Publishing Co., Inc.
New York

Editor-in-chief: *Cristina Sperandeo*
Graphic design: *Paola Masera* and *Amelia Verga*
Translated by *Studio Queens*

Thread color numbers refer to DMC embroidery floss

Library of Congress Cataloging-in-Publication Data Available

10   9   8   7   6   5   4   3   2   1

Published by Sterling Publishing Company, Inc.
387 Park Avenue South, New York, NY 10016
First published in Italy by RCS Libri S.p.A.
under the title *La Biblioteca del Punto Croce—Bordi*
© 1999 RCS Libri S.p.A., Milan 1st Edition Great Fabbri Manuals April 1999
© 2001 English translation by Sterling Publishing Co., Inc.
Distributed in Canada by Sterling Publishing Co., Inc.
c/o Canadian Manda Group, One Atlantic Avenue, Suite 105
Toronto, Onatario, Canada M6K 3E7
Distributed in Great Britain and Europe by Cassell PLC
Wellington House, 125 Strand, London WC2R 0BB, England
Distributed in Australia by Capricorn Link (Australia) Pty Ltd.
P.O. Box 704, Windsor, NSW 2756, Australia

Sterling ISBN 0-8069-7601-2

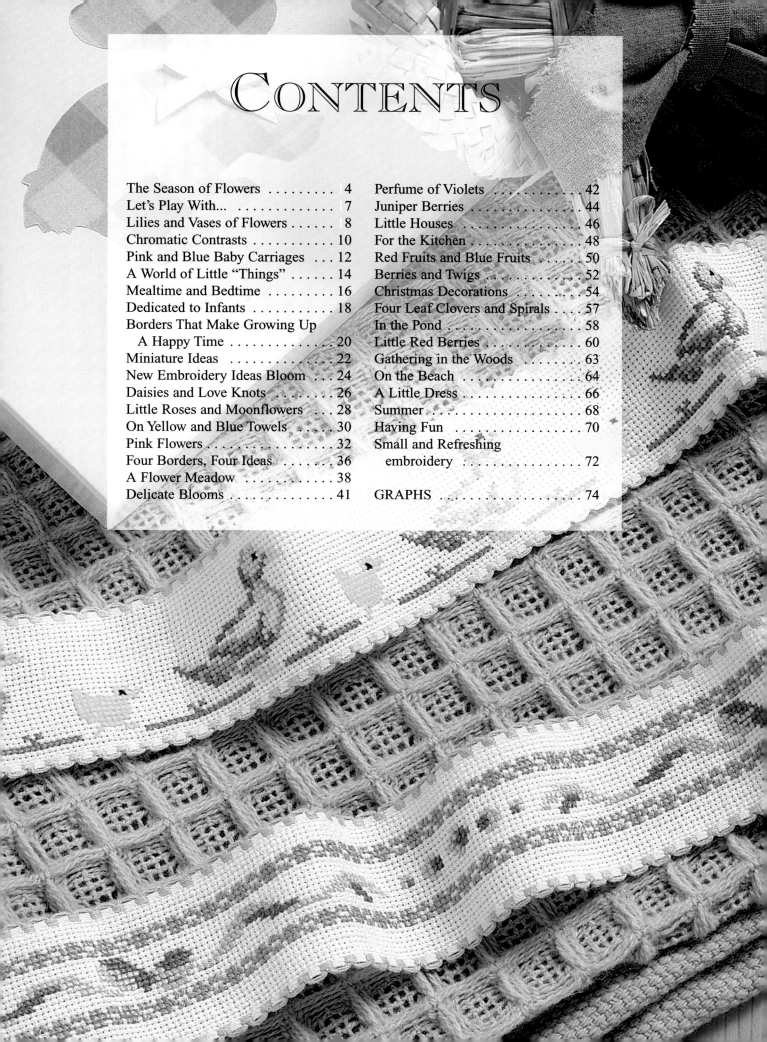

CONTENTS

The Season of Flowers

Spring's explosion of flowers flaunts an infinite array of colors that offer inspiration for embroidering splendid borders to create thousands of ideas!

- cotton Aida borders in white, finished with white edging (distributed by DMC). Width: approx. 4 inches. Length: as needed.

Yellow daisies

- 1 Mouliné DMC floss in each of the following colors:

319	dark pistachio
320	medium pistachio
437	tan medium
741	medium tangerine
743	dark yellow
744	medium yellow
921	light yellow
973	yellow gold
975	golden brown

Orange dahlias

- 1 Mouliné DMC floss in each of the following colors:

444	light yellow gold
606	red orange
740	dark tangerine
3345	dark fern green
3347	medium fern green

Directions

- Cross-stitch each border as laid out in the matching graphs. Repeat each motif until you have reached the desired length.

- At the end of the work, backstitch the indicated lines.

Embroidering

Work the embroidery in cross-stitch using two strands of Mouliné floss following the provided graph and color chart. Each cross-stitch should fill, width-wise and height-wise, one square of Aida canvas. Backstitch using a single strand of Mouliné floss.

■ *The graphs of the motifs are on page 74*

Another Idea

A bloom of perfumed geraniums is one more idea that can be used to decorate the borders of a tablecloth, the bottom of kitchen curtains, or the edges of placemats.

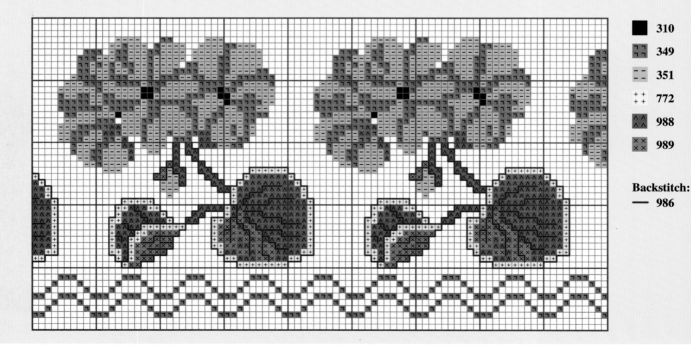

■	310
	349
	351
+ +	772
∧ ∧	988
× ×	989

Backstitch:
— 986

Embroidering

Work the embroidery in cross-stitch using two strands of Moulinè floss following the provided graph and color chart.
Each cross-stitch should fill, width-wise and height-wise, one square of Aida canvas.

Let's Play With...

Jolly motifs to embroider pretty borders that are perfect for decorating objects in a child's room: sheets, the border of a play mat, or bumper pads around a crib.

WHAT YOU NEED

- 2 cotton Aida borders in white, finished with white edging (distributed by DMC). Width: one of 3 inches and one of 4 inches. Length: approx. 64 squares in 4 inches.

- 1 Mouliné DMC floss in each of the following colors:

For the border with swans

91	faded ocean azure
413	light steel gray
444	medium lemon
552	medium violet
606	red orange
702	medium grass green
971	light yellow
3823	very light yellow

On the right: graph of the safety pin motif. Below: graph of the swan motif.

For the border with safety pins

318	pearl gray
471	light apple green
604	medium pink
3325	medium light baby blue

Directions

- Work the stitches following the provided graph and color chart. Make sure that the motif is centered vertically and horizontally. Repeat until the desired length is reached.

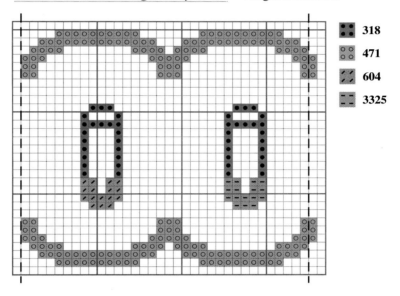

318	
471	
604	
3325	

91	413	444	552	606	702	971	3823

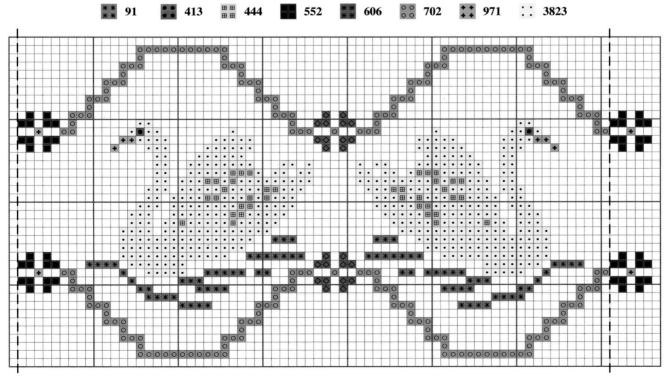

7

Lilies and Vases of Flowers

*Lilies enclosed in scarlet hearts and miniature vases of flowers
centered in medallions are colorful motifs
that are perfect for bathroom accessories and towels.*

Embroidering

Work the embroidery in cross-stitch using two strands of Moulinè floss following the provided graph and color chart. Each cross-stitch should fill, width-wise and height-wise, one square of Aida canvas.

- cotton Aida borders in white, finished with white edging (distributed by DMC). Width: one of 3 inches and one of 4 inches. Length: approx. 66 squares in 4 inches.

- 1 Moulinè DMC floss in each of the following colors:

For the border with lilies

666	bright red
744	medium yellow
792	dark cornflower blue
813	medium delft blue
970	medium yellow
3815	dark olive green
3818	brown green

For the border with vases

444	light lemon
498	garnet

814	dark garnet
909	Christmas green
934	dark forest green
3350	dark antique rose
3778	medium blush

Directions

- Work the stitches following the graph and color chart. Make sure that the motif is centered, vertically and horizontally, and that each motif is the exact distance from the other. Repeat the part between the dotted lines until the desired length is reached.

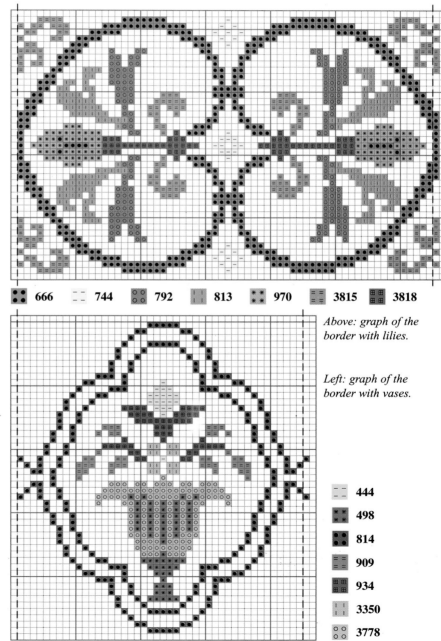

| ●● 666 | ⁻⁻ 744 | ₀₀ 792 | ‖‖ 813 | ✶✶ 970 | ⁼⁼ 3815 | ▦ 3818 |

Above: graph of the border with lilies.

Left: graph of the border with vases.

⁼⁼	444
✶✶	498
●●	814
⁼⁼	909
▦	934
‖‖	3350
₀₀	3778

9

Chromatic Contrasts

The intensity of colors and the playfulness of lines give these borders a jacquard effect that is appropriate for the decoration of tablecloths and accessories for a modern kitchen.

- cotton Aida borders in white, finished with white edging (distributed by DMC). Width: 4 inches. Length: approx. 66 squares in 4 inches.

- 1 Moulinè DMC floss in each of the following colors:

For the border with the petal pattern

307	dark lemon yellow
742	light saffron
796	dark royal blue
3803	dark wine

For the border with the diamond pattern

312	medium blue
702	medium grass green
793	cornflower blue
815	garnet
971	light orange
972	dark gold yellow
3325	medium light baby blue

Directions

- Work the stitches following the graph and color chart. Make sure that the motif is centered, vertically and horizontally, and that each motif is the exact distance from the other. Repeat the part between the dotted lines until the desired length is reached.

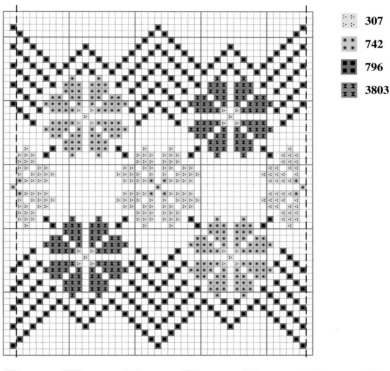

	307
	742
	796
	3803

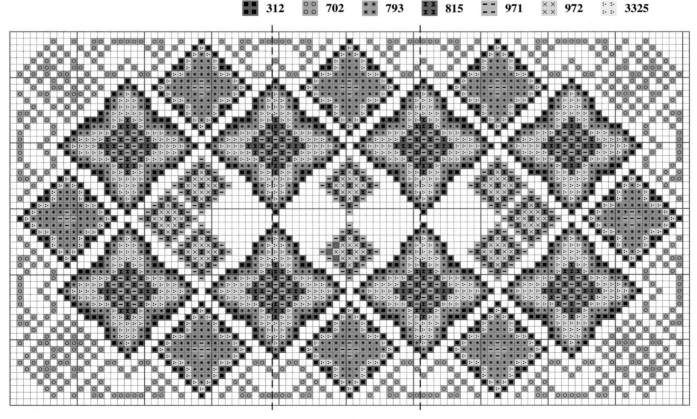

| ■ 312 | ○○ 702 | ✳✳ 793 | ✕✕ 815 | -- 971 | ✕✕ 972 | ∵∵ 3325 |

Pink and Blue Baby Carriages

This border is dedicated to infants and can be applied to baby sheets, crib skirts, and nursery curtains. The same motifs, taken separately, can also be embroidered onto little sachets to give to guests at christenings; pink baby carriages for little girls and blue baby carriages for little boys.

• cotton Aida borders in white, finished with pink ribbon edging (distributed by DMC). Width: approx. 4 inches.

• 1 Moulinè DMC floss in each of the following colors:

318	pearl gray
712	cream
743	very light tangerine
776	medium pink
825	dark royal blue
827	light royal blue
948	light peach
956	dark pink

Directions

• Work the embroidery in cross-stitch and repeat the motifs several times, placing each motif 2 inches from the next until the desired length has been reached. At the end, backstitch the lines indicated on the graph.

Embroidering

Work the embroidery in cross-stitch using two strands of Moulinè floss following the provided graph and color chart. Each cross-stitch should fill, width-wise and height-wise, one square of Aida canvas. Backstitch using only one strand of Moulinè floss.

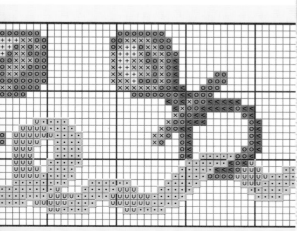

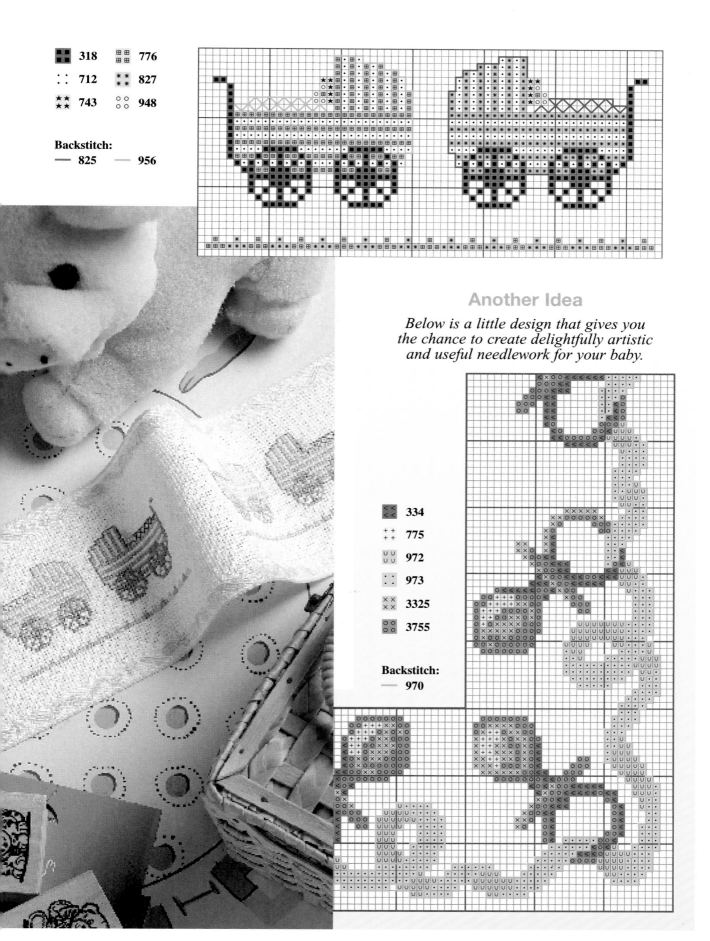

	318		776
	712		827
	743		948

Backstitch:
— 825 — 956

Another Idea

Below is a little design that gives you the chance to create delightfully artistic and useful needlework for your baby.

	334
+ +	775
U U	972
: :	973
X X	3325
o o	3755

Backstitch:
— 970

A World of Little "Things"

Three hearts embroidered on a bib, a border of multicolored dolls, and a cherub shooting an arrow are cute and unusual motifs that can personalize "baby's" little things and render them unique.

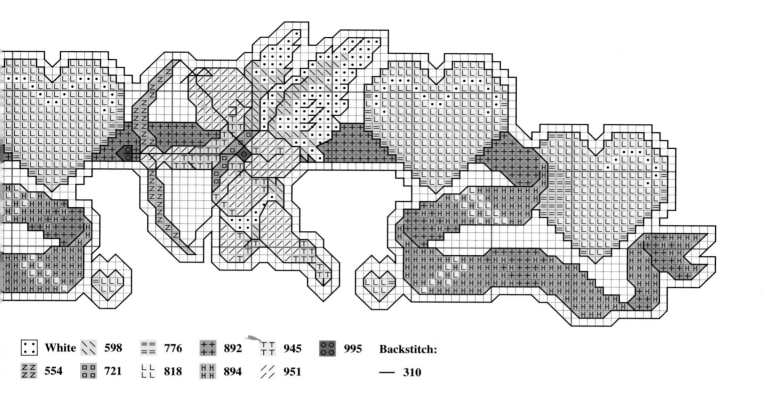

| : : White | \\ 598 | = = 776 | + + 892 | T T 945 | o o 995 | Backstitch: |
| Z Z 554 | o o 721 | L L 818 | H H 894 | // 951 | | — 310 |

• 1 white terrycloth bib with prepared strip in Aida canvas by DMC.

• cotton Aida borders in white, finished with pink ribbon edging (distributed by DMC). Width: one of 4 inches and one of 3 inches. Length: as needed.

• 1 Mouliné DMC floss in each of the following colors:

For the border with the cherubs

	white
310	black
554	dark lavender
598	sky blue
721	medium rust
776	medium pink
818	baby pink
892	petunia
894	pale petunia
945	dark peach flesh
951	sportsman flesh
995	china blue

For the bib

	white
310	black
445	light lemon yellow
747	very light sky blue
799	azure
800	light azure
818	baby pink
819	light baby pink
956	dark confetti pink

For the border with the dolls

310	black
318	pearl gray
350	coral
445	light lemon yellow
600	dark fuchsia
602	fuchsia
741	medium tangerine
815	garnet
817	scarlet
818	baby pink
829	dark old brass
838	very dark beige brown
971	light orange
3820	amber
3821	medium amber

Directions

• Embroider the three hearts making sure to, vertically and horizontally, center them on the strip of Aida canvas. Work the embroidery of the cherub motif on the 4-inch border, and the doll motif on the 3-inch border. Make sure that these are also centered in the middle (vertically and horizontally). Repeat the motifs until you have reached the desired length. Finish off each motif with backstitching following the guidelines indicated on the graphs.

■ The graphs of the bib and doll borders are on page 75

Mealtime and Bedtime

The cricket and the ant are the stars of the timeless fable that can be told to children as a bedtime story, or to keep them amused at mealtimes.

• cotton Aida borders in white, finished with wavy pink or yellow edging (distributed by DMC). Width: 4 inches. Length: as needed.

• 1 Moulinè DMC floss in each of the following colors:

The cricket

	white
	white
209	medium lavender
310	black
311	blue
503	blue green
701	grass green
726	light gold
798	dark azure
799	azure
899	medium rose
963	pale confetti pink

The ant

310	black
347	dark geranium
349	dark coral
367	pistachio
420	golden brown
422	light golden brown
503	blue green
701	grass green
742	light saffron
743	very light tangerine
776	medium pink
818	baby pink
869	hazelnut brown

Directions

• Work the embroidery in cross-stitch and repeat the motifs several times, placing each motif between 1 to 2 inches from the other until the desired length has been reached. At the end, backstitch the lines indicated on the graph.

■ *Graphs of the motifs are on page 76*

Work the embroidery in cross-stitch using two strands of Mouliné floss. Each cross-stitch should fill, width-wise and height-wise, one square of Aida canvas.
For the backstitch, use one or two strands of Mouliné floss as indicated on the provided graph and color chart.

Another Idea

With the alternative charts...

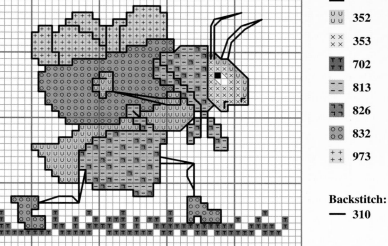

■	310
⊔⊔	352
××	353
TT	702
--	813
⊡⊡	826
○○	832
++	973

Backstitch:
— 310

■	310
⊡⊡	666
⊔⊔	721
++	725
--	783
○○	911
××	3755

Backstitch:
— 310

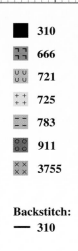

... a set for mealtimes

You will need a napkin in Aida canvas and a terrycloth bib with a prepared strip in Aida canvas. Then you need the Mouliné floss in the colors indicated in the color chart beside the graph on this page. Position the ant with the sack on her back on the bib's Aida border, repeating the motif twice. Position the embroidered "squirrel gardener" on the top left corner of the napkin at approx. 2 inches from the edge.

Dedicated to Infants

Precious borders that make baby is things cheerful and sentimental. Little blue ducklings and yellow chicks run after each other on the first border. On the second, light blue bows are enclosed within two Grecian borders in a tone-on-tone embroidery.

- cotton Aida borders in white, finished with light blue scalloped edging (distributed by DMC). Width: 2 inches. Length: as needed.

- 1 Moulinè DMC floss in each of the following colors:

For the ducks and chicks

307	dark lemon yellow
310	black
444	medium lemon
519	medium aqua blue
700	dark grass green
3760	dark aqua blue
3761	light aqua blue

For the bows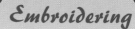

519	medium aqua blue
3760	dark aqua blue
3761	light aqua blue

Directions

- Work the embroidery in cross-stitch making sure to vertically center the motif. Repeat it several times until the desired length has been reached.

■ *Graph of the motif is on page 77*

Embroidering

Work the embroidery in cross-stitch using two strands of Moulinè floss following the provided graph and color chart. Each cross-stitch should fill, width-wise and height-wise, one square of Aida canvas.

∕∕	307	✕✕	519	ʟʟ	3761
■	310	╫	700		
═	444	⚏	3760		

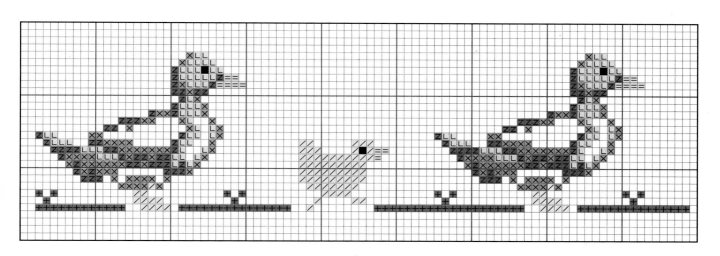

Another Idea

A family of rooster, hen, little chicks, and a Setter make great borders for baby's outfits.

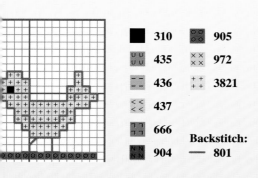

■	310	⊙⊙	905
ᴜᴜ	435	✕✕	972
⚌	436	⁺⁺	3821
≺≺	437		
⚏	666	**Backstitch:**
ɴɴ	904	— 801

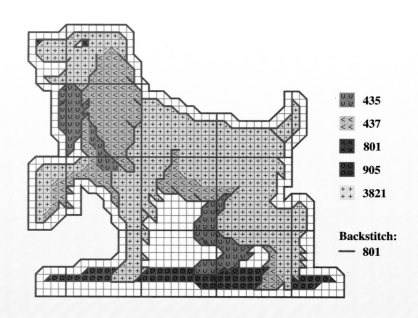

ᴜᴜ	435
≺≺	437
✕✕	801
⊙⊙	905
⁺⁺	3821

Backstitch:
— 801

Borders That Make Growing Up A Happy Time

Cute and colorful little men and women line these borders that can be used to decorate many things. Two cups of deliciously inviting ice cream decorate the border of a bib.

Embroidering

Work the embroidery in cross-stitch and French knots using two strands of Mouliné floss. Each cross-stitch should fill, width-wise and height-wise, one square of Aida canvas. Follow the instructions laid out on the provided graph and color chart. Finish off in backstitch as indicated on the graph.

For the border with ice cream

- 1 white terrycloth bib (distributed by DMC), ready to embroider, with a pre-pared strip in Aida canvas of 2 inches with approx. 66 squares in 4 inches.

304	dark red
310	black
543	pink beige
666	bright red
676	wheat
729	dark old gold
829	dark old brass
842	light beige brown
911	emerald green
913	light emerald green
931	antique blue
932	light antique blue

3341	light apricot
3824	pale apricot

For the border with the little men and women

- cotton Aida borders in white, finished with pink edging (distributed by DMC). Width: 3 inches with approx. 60 squares in 4 inches. Length: as needed.

- 1 Mouliné DMC floss in each of the following colors:

310	black
322	light blue
334	dark sky blue
335	light cranberry
760	dark salmon
776	medium pink
829	dark old brass

899	medium rose
905	dark lime green
3328	light red
3752	light powder blue
3820	amber
3821	medium amber
3824	pale apricot

Directions

- Work the embroidery in cross-stitch following the provided graph and color chart. Begin with the center of the motif making sure that it corresponds to the vertical and horizontal center of the Aida border or the Aida strip. For the border, repeat the motifs until the desired length has been reached. For the bib, work the motif as laid out. At the end, finish off the motif in backstitch and French knots as indicated on the graph.

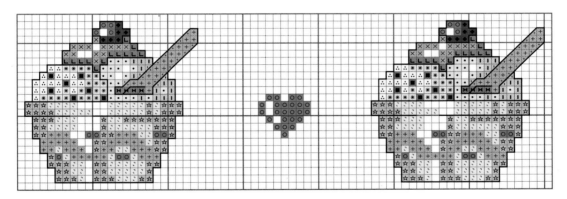

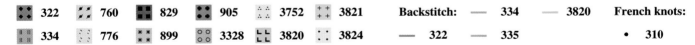

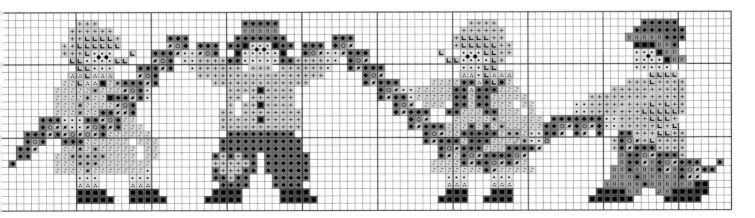

21

Miniature Ideas

These little motifs can be embroidered on pillowcases, crib covers, and sheets. They also could be separately embroidered onto slippers or hats. They are great for little boys and girls' clothing.

- cotton Aida cloth border in white, finished with pink edging (distributed by DMC). Width: 3 inches with approx. 55 squares in 4 inches. Length: as needed.

- 1 Moulinè DMC floss in each of the following colors:

Little horse motif

310	black
517	dark sky blue
725	dark honey
976	medium golden brown
3761	light aqua blue

Little duck motif

741	dark sun yellow
761	salmon
3041	sun yellow

Little bird motif

553	lilac
726	honey
747	pale aqua blue
3716	light pink
3743	very light amethyst

Little bear motif

310	black
435	dark tan
437	medium tan
543	pink beige
3716	light pink
3810	light peacock blue
3811	medium opal

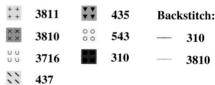

Embroidering

Work the embroidery in cross-stitch using two strands of Moulinè floss. Each cross-stitch should fill, width-wise and height-wise, one square of Aida canvas. Follow the indications laid out on the provided graph and color chart. The backstitch requires one strand of Moulinè floss. For the little bear, follow the graph printed on this page.

++	3811	▼▼	435	**Backstitch:**
××	3810	○○	543	— 310
UU	3716	✚	310	— 3810
＼＼	437			

■ *Graphs of the motifs are on page 78*

22

Another Idea

A bib with ruffles

What you need

- 10 x 9 inch Aida canvas (distributed by DMC) with 55 squares in 4 inches
- 10 x 9 inches of felt fabric
- 59 inches of print ribbon with a width of 2 inches
- Moulinè floss in each of the colors indicated in the color chart beside the graph
- one small button

Directions

Adjust the chart into the desired dimensions using tracing paper. Pin the tracing paper to both fabrics and cut, allowing an 0.4 inch for turning under. Embroider the motif at the exact center of the Aida. Gather the ribbon until you have reached the length of the circumference of the bib. Place one bib over the other, with the right sides together and the ruffles in between, and sew the edges together leaving an opening. Turn inside out and sew up the opening. Make a buttonhole on one side of the neckline and sew the button on the other side.

Graph of bib

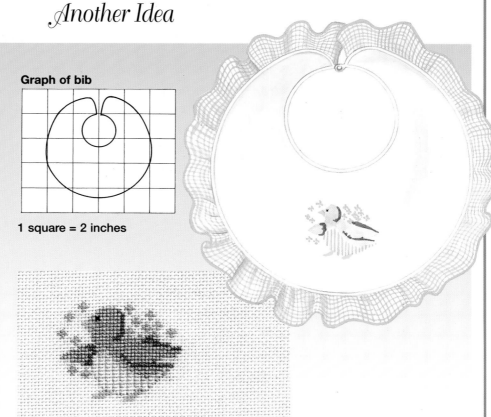

1 square = 2 inches

Tunic

What you need

- 1 rectangle of Aida canvas (distributed by DMC) of 30 x 10 inches with 55 squares in 4 inches • 1 strip of print fabric 100 x 3 inches • 2 strips of print fabric 50 x 3 inches • 40 inches of ribbon with a 1-inch width • 1 small button

Directions

Adjust the chart into the desired dimensions using tracing paper. Fold the Aida canvas and pin the center front onto the folded line and the remaining back part. Cut, allowing an 0.4 inch, along all the borders. Work the embroidery on the front at approx. 2 inches from the bottom. Sew the shoulders and turn back the edges on the reverse side at the dotted line. Sew a finished 0.4 inch hemline on the outside edge of the strips and ruffles on the front and back. Finish off the sides with a hem, and finish the neckline by sewing bias tape along the edges as a border. Make a buttonhole and sew the button on the other side. To make the side fastenings, sew four 10-inch pieces of ribbon near the beginning of the ruffles.

1 square = 2 inches

Graph of tunic

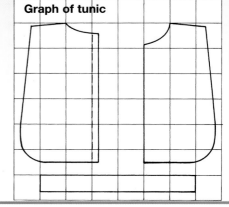

New Embroidery Ideas Bloom

Floral decorations bloom on these borders that can be sewn onto lingerie or bed linens. On the first border, there is a chain of flowers and on the second, more flowers are entwined with laced ribbons.

Embroidering

Work the embroidery in cross-stitch using two strands of Mouliné floss. Follow the instructions laid out on the provided graph and color chart. Each cross-stitch should fill, width-wise and height-wise, one square of Aida. The backstitch requires only one strand of Mouliné floss.

- cotton Aida borders in ivory, finished with ivory scalloped edging (distributed by DMC). Width: 2 inches. Length: as needed.

For the border with flowers

- Mouliné DMC floss in each of the following colors:

307	dark lemon yellow
349	dark coral
352	salmon
754	light salmon
772	pale pine green
935	dark avocado green
976	medium golden brown
3052	olive green

For the border with flowers and ribbons

- 1 Mouliné DMC floss in each of the following colors:

307	dark lemon yellow
349	dark coral
352	salmon
754	light salmon
976	medium golden brown
3052	olive green

Directions

- Embroider in cross-stitch vertically centering each motif on the border. Repeat the motifs until the desired length has been reached. At the end, finish off the motifs in backstitch according to the provided graphs.

■ *Graphs of the motifs are on page 77*

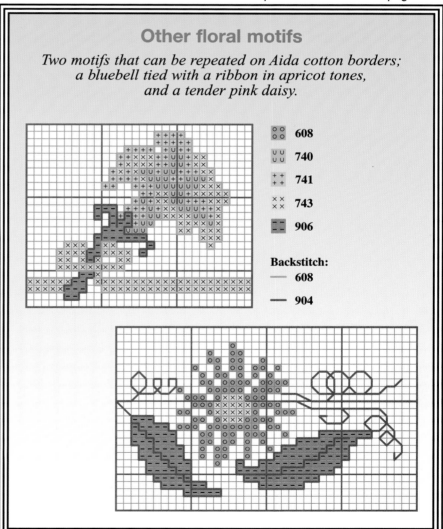

Other floral motifs

Two motifs that can be repeated on Aida cotton borders; a bluebell tied with a ribbon in apricot tones, and a tender pink daisy.

oo / oo	608
U U / U U	740
++ / ++	741
×× / ××	743
▬▬ / ▬▬	906

Backstitch:

—	608
▬	904

Daisies and Love Knots

A bunch of flowers tied with ribbon. This is an idea for two borders, or for the creation of more original and imaginative needlework. You can even embroider one single bunch of blue or yellow daisies and then display it in a small fabric-coated frame.

- cotton Aida borders in ivory, finished with scalloped edging (distributed by DMC). Width: approx. 4 inches. Length: as needed

- 8 x 8 inch Aida ivory canvas with approx. 55 squares in 4 inches (for the work to frame)

- 1 Mouliné DMC floss in each of the following colors:

Border with blue flowers

307	dark lemon yellow
727	light gold
826	sky blue
827	light sky blue
3364	light pine green
3815	dark olive green
3816	medium olive green
3817	light olive green
3820	amber
3821	medium amber

Border with yellow flowers

307	dark lemon yellow
498	light wine
727	light gold
813	medium sky blue
825	dark sky blue
827	light sky blue
3815	dark olive green
3816	medium olive green
3820	amber
3821	medium amber

- 1 small frame covered in blue and white-striped fabric with an opening the size of the embroidery

- 1 small sheet of cardboard to fit the frame

- glue for textiles

■ *Graphs of border are on page 79*

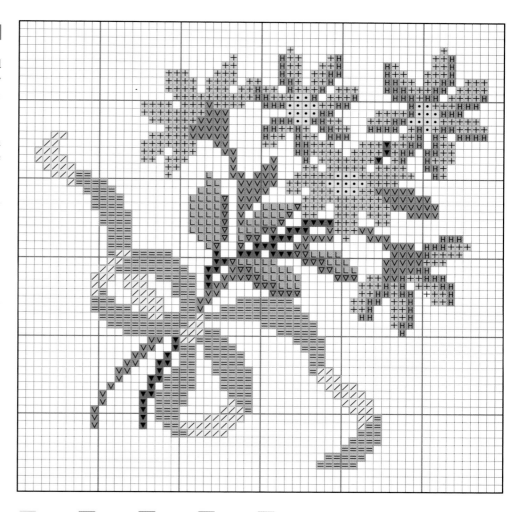

::	307	HH	826	VV	3364	VV	3816	==	3821		Backstitch:
//	727	++	827	▼▼	3815	LL	3817			—	3820

Directions

- **For the border with blue flowers:** center the motifs on the border and repeat until the desired length is reached.

- **For the border with yellow flowers:** center the motifs on the border, alternating one bunch with light yellow flowers and one bunch with darker yellow flowers. Repeat until the desired length is reached.

- **For the creation of the picture frame:** embroider a bunch of yellow flowers (or whatever you prefer) in the center of the Aida canvas. Iron the fabric on the wrong side and starch. Glue the fabric onto the cardboard taking care to place it in the exact center. Cut away excess fabric and insert it into the frame.

BACKSTITCH

With one strand of Mouliné floss, work a line of backstitches making a stitch forward and a stitch back, and by taking and skipping one square of Aida each time.

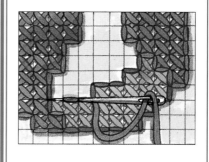

Little Roses and Moonflowers

You can embroider these onto two borders to perk up a country style cupboard.

WHAT YOU NEED

• cotton Aida borders in white, finished with a white-dotted edging (distributed by DMC). Width: approx. 4 inches. Length: as needed.
• 1 Moulinè DMC floss in each of the following colors:

For the moonflowers

341	lavender
726	honey
793	medium blue
794	light blue
905	dark lime green
907	light lime green

For the little roses

349	dark geranium
350	coral
352	salmon
353	medium salmon
905	dark lime green
907	light lime green

Directions

• Work the embroidery taking care to vertically center the motif on the border. Repeat until the desired length has been reached.

Embroidering

Work the embroidery in cross-stitch using two strands of Moulinè floss following the provided graph and color chart. Each cross-stitch should fill, width-wise and height-wise, one square of Aida canvas.

■ *Graphs of the motifs are on page 80*

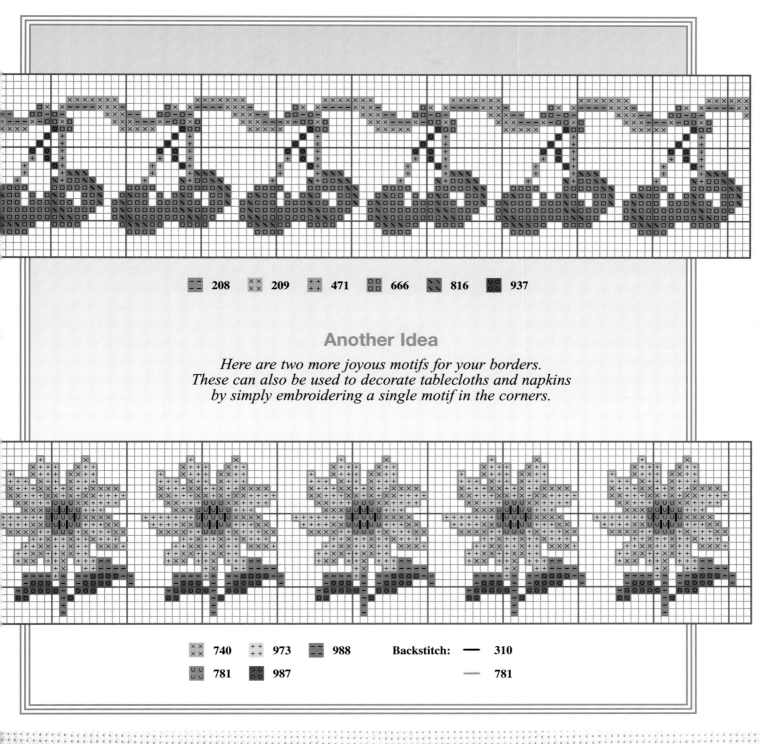

	208		209		471		666		816		937

Another Idea

Here are two more joyous motifs for your borders.
These can also be used to decorate tablecloths and napkins
by simply embroidering a single motif in the corners.

	740		973		988	Backstitch:	——	310
	781		987			——	781

On Yellow and Blue Towels

Blue flowers tied with a ribbon for the blue towel, and bouquets of yellow flowers for the yellow towel are perfect bathroom ideas. The same motifs can be used to create a personal set of bathroom accessories.

Embroidering

Work the embroidery in cross-stitch using two strands of Mouliné floss following the provided graph and color chart. Each cross-stitch should fill, width-wise and height-wise, one square of Aida canvas. The backstitch requires only one strand of Mouliné floss.

For the border with blue flowers

• cotton Aida borders in white, finished with white bow edging (distributed by DMC). Width: approx. 4 inches. Length: as needed.

• 1 Mouliné DMC floss in each of the following colors:

350	coral
352	salmone
704	pale grass green
726	light gold
797	light royal blue
798	dark azure
809	medium azure
815	garnet
899	medium rose
909	dark emerald green
911	emerald green
954	light Nile green
963	light rose
3818	brown green

■ Graph of one motif is on page 81

For the border with yellow flowers

• cotton Aida borders in white, finished with yellow-dotted edging (distributed by DMC). Width: approx. 4 inches. Length: as needed.

• 1 Mouliné DMC floss in each of the following colors:

304	dark red
307	dark lemon yellow
986	very dark leaf green
987	dark leaf green
988	medium leaf green
989	light leaf green
3078	light lemon yellow
3340	apricot

Directions

• Work the embroidery in cross-stitch following the graph for each border. At the end, embroider the lines indicated in backstitch.

350		726		815		911		**Backstitch:**		
352		798		899		954		— 350	— 815	
704		809		909		963		— 797	— 3818	

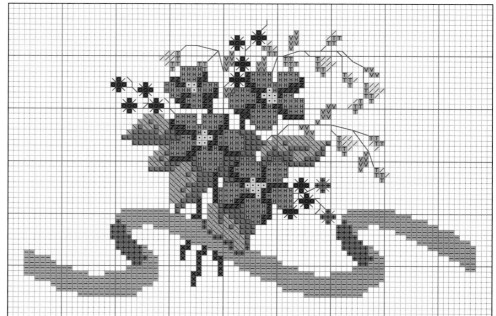

Pink Flowers

Floral patterns in pastel tones are ideal for bordering curtains, sheets, or bath linens.

- cotton Aida borders in beige, finished with scalloped edging (distributed by DMC) with approx. 56 squares in 4 inches. Length: as needed.

- 1 Moulinè DMC floss in each of the following colors:

For the border with pink flowers

322	light blue
369	verde bottiglia pallido
632	dark walnut
721	peach
754	light salmon
780	dark mustard
815	garnet
832	light old brass
892	petunia
934	dark avocado green
936	medium avocado green
948	light peach flesh
3345	dark fern green
3347	medium fern green
3348	light fern green
3708	carnation red
3825	light peach

For the border with salmon flowers

334	dark sky blue
336	dark blue
356	dark pink beige
407	nut
604	medium pink
741	dark sun yellow
745	light yellow
758	light terra cotta
832	light old brass
833	light golden olive
900	dark orange
934	dark avocado green
936	avocado green
950	light sportsman flesh
988	leaf green
3013	light moss green
3348	light olive
3774	pearl beige
3825	light peach

Directions

- Work the embroidery in cross-stitch following the graph and color chart for each border. Repeat the motif until you have reached the desired length. For the border with the salmon flowers, do the first part repeating the section found within the dotted lines as many times as needed, then complete by following the graph for the final section.

Embroidering

Work the embroidery in cross-stitch using two strands of Moulinè floss following the provided graph and color chart. Each cross-stitch should fill, width-wise and height-wise, one square of Aida canvas.

Border with salmon flowers

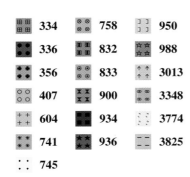

⊞	334	⊗	758	⌐	950
●	336	▥	832	☆	988
◆	356	◉	833	↑	3013
○	407	✕	900	⊘	3348
+	604	■	934	⠂	3774
✳	741	★	936	―	3825
∴	745				

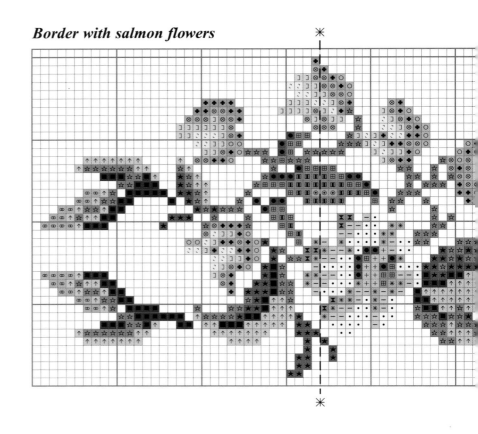

Border with pink flowers

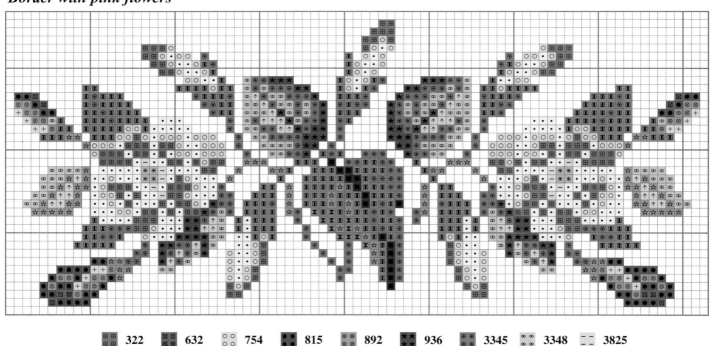

⊞	322	▨	632	○	754	●	815	⊗	892	★	936	◉	3345	⊠	3348	― 3825
↑	369	✳	721	✕	780	▥	832	■	934	∴	948	☆	3347	+	3708	

34

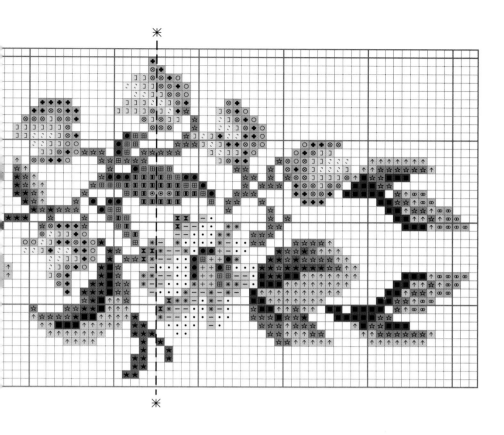

Another Idea

Here is another idea in tones of blue, turquoise, and green that brings a touch of fresh perfume to the countless objects that you can decorate.

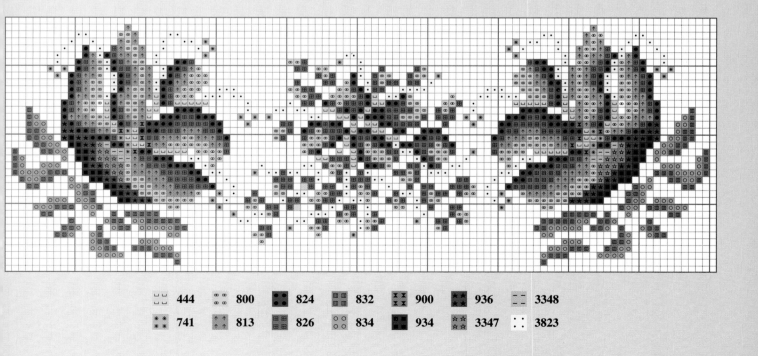

⊔⊔ 444	∞∞ 800	●● 824	⊞⊞ 832	✕✕ 900	★★ 936	⁻⁻ 3348
✱✱ 741	↑↑ 813	⊞⊞ 826	○○ 834	■■ 934	☆☆ 3347	∶∶ 3823

Four Borders, Four Ideas

Four different ideas that are equally elegant and practical: lilies for a blouse, cornflowers for a sheet, poppies for a tea cloth, and snowdrops for a crib coverlet.

Embroidering

Work the embroidery in cross-stitch using two strands of Moulinè floss following the provided graph and color chart. Each cross-stitch should fill, width-wise and height-wise, one square of Aida canvas. The backstitch and the French knots require only one strand of Moulinè floss.

WHAT YOU NEED

• cotton Aida borders in white (distributed by DMC) of 2½ inches (for the poppies and blue flowers) and 3 inches (for the lilies and cornflowers). Length: as needed.
• 1 Moulinè DMC floss in each of the following colors:

Border with lilies

310	black
369	pale pistachio
741	dark sun yellow
743	dark yellow
744	yellow
745	light yellow
819	pale baby pink
977	pumpkin
3346	fern green
3348	light fern green
3805	medium camellia rose
3806	camellia rose

Border with cornflowers

307	dark lemon yellow
772	pale pine green
824	dark sky blue
825	dark royal blue
3813	light sage green
3815	dark olive green

Border with poppies

3801	red
3818	brown green

Border with snowdrops

798	dark azure
809	medium azure

Directions

• Work the embroidery in cross-stitch following the graph and color chart for each border. Make sure the motif is centered. Finish off the motif in backstitch following the guidelines indicated on the graph. Complete the border of lilies by embroidering the pistils in French knots with the color "pumpkin" n. 977.

■ *Graphs of two motifs are on page 81*

36

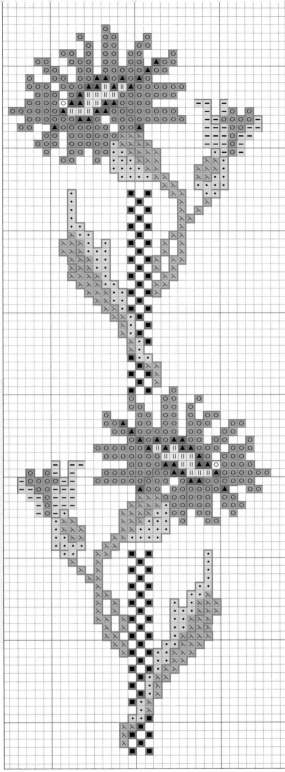

THE FRENCH KNOT

Bring the threaded needle to the right side of the fabric without pulling the needle through. Wind the thread around the needle 3 or 4 times and draw the needle through the knot. Stitch back into the fabric near the starting point, pulling the knot tight.

‖ ‖	307
⋮ ⋮	772
▲ ▲	824
◉ ◉	825
‒ ‒	827
⤬ ⤬	3813
▦ ▦	3815

Backstitch
— 824
— 3815

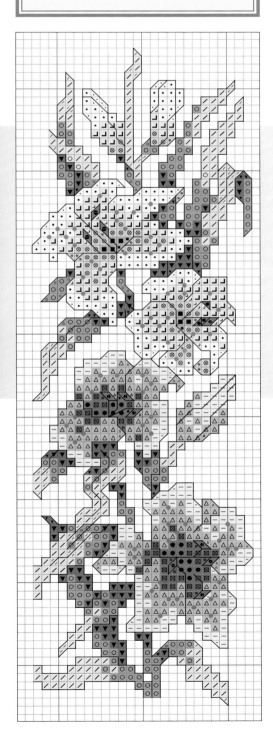

⁄ ⁄	369
▪ ▪	741
⊗ ⊗	743
⌐ ⌐	744
∴ ∴	745
‒ ‒	819
● ●	977
▼ ▼	3346
○ ○	3348
△ △	3805
⊠ ⊠	3806

Backstitch:
— 310

37

A Flower Meadow

The practical advantage of the ready-finished border combines nicely with the elegant floral motifs. The designs are nosegays enhanced by backstitching.

- cotton Aida borders in white (distributed by DMC). Width: 4 inches with 60 squares in 4 inches. Length: as needed.

- 1 Moulinè DMC floss in each of the following colors:

Border with bluebells

310	black
350	dark salmon
351	salmon
352	light salmon
402	light orange
502	dark blue green
503	blue green
504	light blue green
721	medium rust
722	light rust
904	dark lime green
906	medium lime green
945	dark peach flesh
951	sportsman flesh
3078	pale yellow
3773	dark pink

Border with moonflowers

368	pistachio
369	light pistachio
519	medium aqua blue
553	violet
554	light violet
3760	dark aqua blue
3815	dark olive green
3817	light olive green
3819	light avocado green

Border with roses

562	medium jade green
742	sun yellow
746	ivory
3761	light aqua blue
3808	dark peacock blue
3810	light peacock blue
3815	dark olive green
3817	light olive green
3820	dark amber
3821	medium amber
3822	light amber

PLEASE DON'T PICK THE FLOWERS

Embroidering

Work the embroidery in cross-stitch using two strands of Moulinè floss following the provided graph and color chart. Each cross-stitch should fill, width-wise and height-wise, one square of Aida canvas. For the straight stitch, two strands of Moulinè floss are used, while the backstitch requires only one strand of Moulinè floss.

■ *Graph of the motif is on page 86*

STRAIGHT STITCH

Take long stitches that cover the indicated lines. Bring the needle up through the fabric at the beginning of the stitch and insert it back into the fabric at the end of the line to be covered by the stitch.

368
369
519
554
3760
3817
3819

Backstitch:
553
3760
3815

	310		402		504		906		3078	Backstitch:		721
	351		502		722		945				310		904
	352		503		904		951				350		3773

Delicate Blooms

Two borders of elegant posies in tones of pink and yellow add a touch of romance to your bedroom.

Embroidering

Work the embroidery in cross-stitch using two strands of Moulinè floss following the provided graph and color chart. Each cross-stitch should fill, width-wise and height-wise, one square of Aida canvas. The backstitch requires only one strand of Moulinè floss.

WHAT YOU NEED

• cotton Aida borders in white, finished with a yellow ribbon edging (distributed by DMC). Width: approx. 4 inches. Length: as needed.

• Moulinè DMC floss in each of the following colors:

For the border with yellow flowers

471	light apple green
561	medium jade green
562	light jade green
782	medium gold
973	yellow gold
3820	amber

For the border with pink flowers

221	dark shell pink
561	medium jade green
562	light jade green
776	medium pink
899	medium rose
973	yellow gold

Directions

• Work embroidery in cross-stitch vertically centering the motif and following, for each border, the relative graph and color chart provided. Repeat each motif lengthways at a distance of approx. 4 inches from the other until you have reached the desired length.

■ *Graphs of the motifs are on pages 82 and 83.*

Another Idea

Pillows and headboard

With two strands of Moulinè floss, cross-stitch the border design to frame the edges of four linen pillowcases with approx. 110 threads in 4 inches. Pick up two threads, both vertically and horizontally, of fabric for each cross-stitch. Follow the graph and color chart printed on this page. At the end, sew ribbons in the same color to the upper corners of two of the pillowcases. Insert pillows and tie the ribbons in bows to the upper bar of the headboard. Insert pillows into the remaining pillowcases.

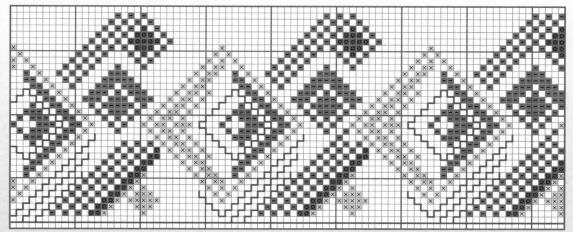

▨	911
▣	699
✕	954

Backstitch:
— 699

Perfume of Violets

Three nosegays of violets bloom on the border around the yoke of a nightgown in print fabric.

Embroidering

Work the embroidery in cross-stitch using two strands of Mouliné floss following the provided graph and color chart. Each cross-stitch should fill, width-wise and height-wise, one square of Aida canvas.

- cotton Aida borders in white, finished with pink edging (distributed by DMC). Width: 4 inches with approx. 62 squares in 4 inches. Length: 40 inches.

- 1 Moulinè DMC floss in each of the following colors:

208	dark lavender
209	medium lavender
327	dark pink
743	very light tangerine
745	light yellow
3345	dark fern green
3347	medium fern green
3348	light fern green

- 1 spool of DMC Filomax in white

- 1 cotton nightgown in a pink print with a square collar

Directions

- Work the embroidery in cross-stitch as follows: Establish the center of the border and, starting in this point, cross-stitch the central flower following the graph provided. On the left and on the right of the flower, work the corner motifs keeping in mind that the dotted lines indicate the point in which the border will be folded to form the corner. (The part of the border that remains empty corresponds to the part that will be turned under.)

Finishing

- At the end, complete the embroidery by working the lines indicated in backstitch. Form the corners by folding the border indicated by the dotted lines. Pin the border to the neckline, back and front, and machine sew with Filomax thread.

■ *Graphs of the motifs are on pages 84 and 85*

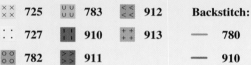

						Backstitch:	
××	725	UU	783	<<	912	—	780
∴	727	▮▮	910	++	913	—	910
∘∘	782	⟩⟩	911				

Another Idea

Use other flowers and other perfumes to repeat on the borders or to embroider instead of the violets.
To make the corners, follow the procedure indicated in the explanation here and on pages 84 and 85.

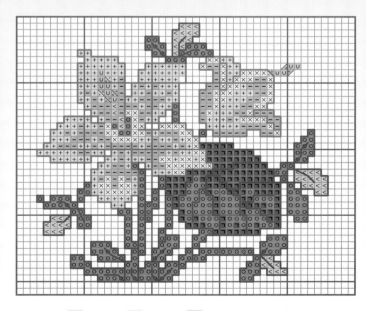

						Backstitch:	
— —	209	<<	472	∘∘	906		
++	210	UU	741			—	552
××	211	▮▮	905			—	904

Juniper Berries

*Here is a little motif to stitch or embroider on small curtains,
or on the center of a tablecloth.*

WHAT YOU NEED

- cotton Aida borders in white, finished with a white bow edging (distributed by DMC). Width: 4 inches. Length: as needed.

- 1 Mouliné DMC floss in each of the following colors:

791	*dark blue*
986	*dark leaf green*
988	*leaf green*
3807	*blue*

Directions

- Work the embroidery in cross-stitch on the Aida border making sure that it is vertically and horizontally centered. Repeat until the desired length has been reached.

■ *Graph of the motif is on page 86*

Embroidering

Work the embroidery in cross-stitch using two strands of Mouliné floss following the provided graph and color chart. Each cross-stitch should fill, width-wise and height-wise, one square of Aida canvas.

Another Idea

Poinsettias along a ribbon embellished with delicate bows, and a posy of golden berries is another motif to embroider.

○○	732	××	906	
<<	900	++	971	
⊐⊏	905			

⊐⊏	321	<<	971
××	472	**Backstitch:**	
++	725	—	781
⊐⊏	783	—	902
UU	906	—	936

Little Houses

Embroidery inspired by the loveliest fables.
*The house with the little hearts looks a lot like the gingerbread house in **Hanzel and Gretel**,*
while the mushroom house seems to come directly out of a cartoon.

- cotton Aida borders in white, finished with red-dotted edging (distributed by DMC). Width: 4 inches. Length: as needed.

- 1 Moulinè DMC floss in each of the following colors:

For the border with the little houses with hearts:

310	black
433	cacao
498	garnet
666	bright red
700	dark grass green
704	pale grass green
727	light honey
976	dark pumpkin
3326	dark pearl pink

For the border with mushroom houses

310	black
415	medium pearl gray
433	cacao
445	lemon yellow
498	garnet
666	bright red
700	dark grass green
704	pale grass green
725	dark honey
727	light honey
976	dark pumpkin
3326	dark pearl pink

Directions

- Embroider making sure that the motif is centered on the border. Repeat each motif until the desired size is reached. At the end, finish off the wooden fences of the houses in French knots following the instructions given on the side.

Embroidering

Work the embroidery in cross-stitch using two strands of Moulinè floss following the provided graph and color chart. Each cross-stitch should fill, width-wise and height-wise, one square of Aida canvas. Use only one strand for French knots.

■ *Graphs of the motifs are on page 87*

Graphs of the motifs are on page 87

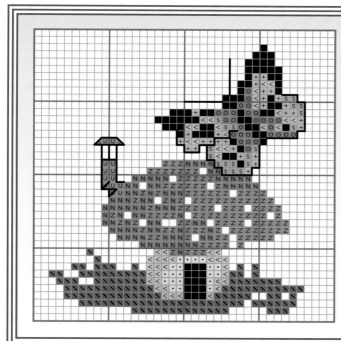

Other funny houses

There's the snail that carries her house on her back, and a small mushroom where a butterfly has chosen to live. These are easy and pleasant motifs that can be embroidered onto a baby's bib, linen set, or crib sheets.

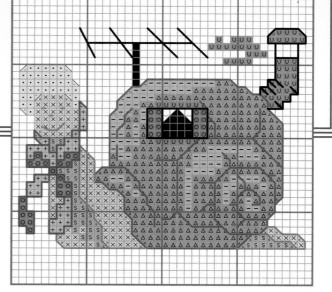

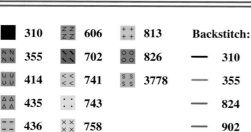

■	310	ZZ	606	++	813	**Backstitch:**	
NN	355	NN	702	OO	826	—	310
UU	414	<<	741	SS	3778	—	355
▲▲	435	::	743			—	824
--	436	XX	758			—	902

For the Kitchen

Whether it is on shelves, fireplace mantels, or curtains, these mixed fruits can be quickly embroidered in Perlè floss to give the kitchen a cheerful, new touch.

Embroidering

Work the embroidery in cross-stitch using the Perlè floss following the provided graph and color chart. Each cross-stitch will vertically and horizontally cross two threads of fabric.

48

Border with bowls of fruit

• 20 x 6 inches of Davosa cloth in pink with approx. 70 threads in 4 inches (distributed by DMC) for each strip.

• 1 Perlè DMC n. 5 floss in each of the following colors:

317	light steel gray
318	pearl gray
471	light yellow green
472	light apple green
666	bright red
743	dark yellow
745	light yellow
762	light pearl gray
783	gold
3326	dark pearl pink

• 1 Moulinè DMC floss in each of the following colors:

414	dark pearl gray
300	dark brick
3363	pine green
3799	steel gray

Border with strawberries and cherries

• 1 Perlè DMC n. 5 floss in each of the following colors:

321	dark red
471	light yellow green
744	yellow
815	garnet
898	dark brown
3326	dark pearl pink

Directions

• Work the embroidery making sure that the motif is vertically and horizontally centered on the fabric. Finish off the border with the bowls of fruit by embroidering the lines, indicated on the graph in backstitch using two threads of Moulinè floss.

■ *Graphs of the motifs are on page 88*

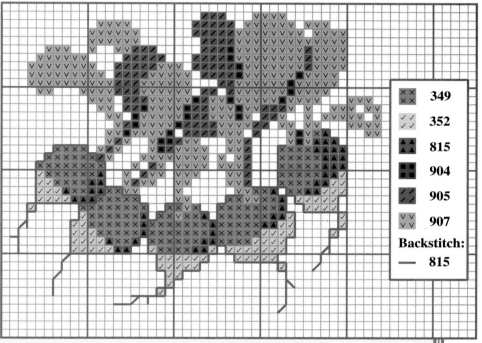

	349
✗✗	349
✓✓	352
▲▲	815
■■	904
◫◫	905
˅˅	907
Backstitch:	
—	815

Another Idea

✗✗	349
✓✓	352
▫▫	676
✳✳	782
▲▲	815
◫◫	905
˅˅	907
Backstitch:	
—	815

Cheerful radishes in bunches, or scattered along a border can decorate oven mitts, aprons, dishcloths, or curtains...

Red Fruits and Blue Fruits

Cherries and blueberries embroidered on borders can be used to label jars of jam, which make a great gift.

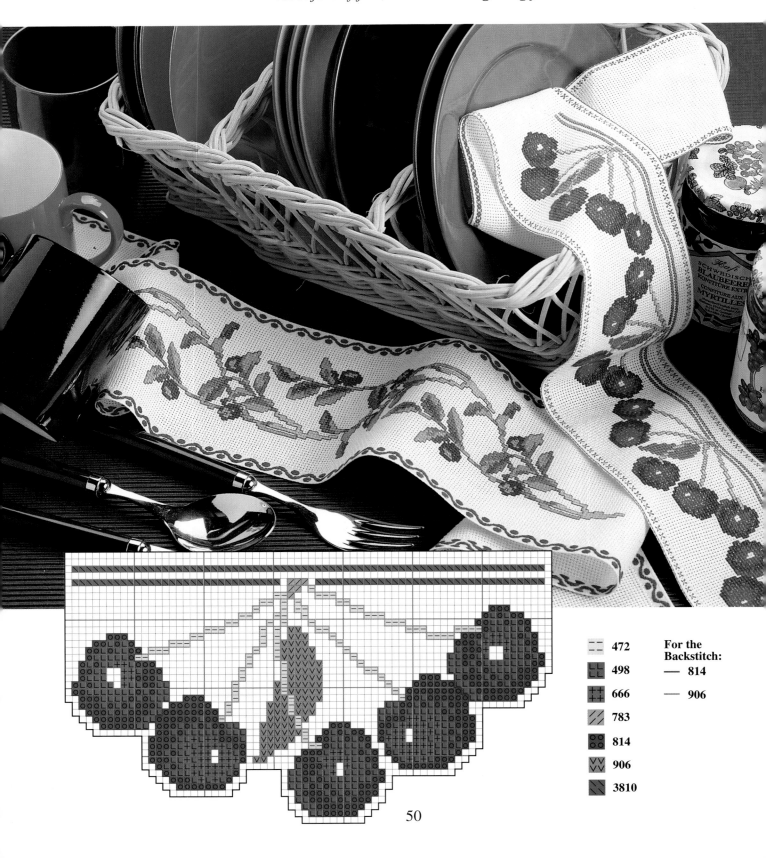

472	
498	
666	
783	
814	
906	
3810	

For the Backstitch:
— 814
— 906

- cotton Aida borders in white, finished with a dotted-red and wavy blue edging (distributed by DMC). Width: 4 inches. Length: as needed.

- 1 Mouliné DMC floss in each of the following colors:

For the cherry border

472	light apple green
498	garnet
666	bright red
783	gold
814	dark garnet
906	lime green
3810	light peacock blue

For the blueberry border

472	light apple green
796	royal blue
809	medium azure
905	dark lime green
907	light lime green
986	dark leaf green

- glue for fabrics

Directions

- Work the embroidery in cross-stitch following, for each border, the provided graph and color chart. Repeat each motif until you have achieved the desired length. At the end, work the lines indicated on the graph in backstitch.

- Cut the borders to the size of the circumference of the jars allowing an extra 1-inch for folding. Apply the borders to the respective jars with a few drops of glue after having turned back the surplus fabric.

■ *Graph of the motif is on page 89*

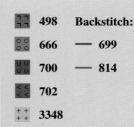

Embroidering

Work the embroidery in cross-stitch using two strands of Mouliné floss following the provided graph and color chart. Each cross-stitch should fill, width-wise and height-wise, one square of Aida canvas. The backstitch requires only one strand of Mouliné floss.

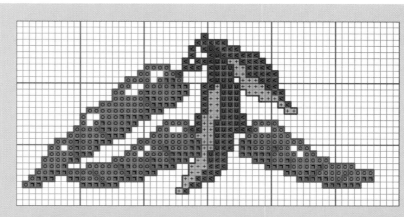

::	352		702	
××	353			
	498	Backstitch:		
°°	666	—	699	
∪∪	700	—	814	

	498	Backstitch:		
°°	666	—	699	
∪∪	700	—	814	
<<	702			
++	3348			

Another Idea

Peppers and strawberries are two other motifs dedicated to making jam and preserves. They can also be embroidered on to; dish towels, potholders, oven mitts, and aprons.

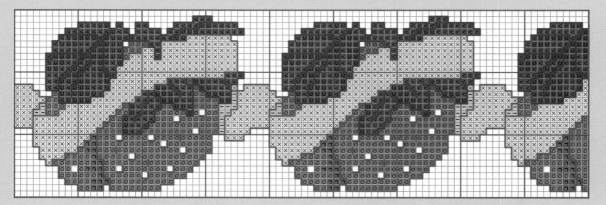

51

Berries and Twigs

*Santa Claus and a little bird are two delightful border motifs that
can create original tray linings or tie backs for curtains.*

Embroidering

Work the embroidery in
cross-stitch using two
strands of Mouliné floss
following the provided
graph and color chart.
Each cross-stitch should
fill, width-wise and
height-wise, one square
of Aida canvas.
The backstitch requires
only one strand of
Mouliné floss.

Border with Santa Claus

- cotton Aida borders in white, finished with a red-scalloped edging (distributed by DMC). Width: 2 inches. Length: 51 inches.

- 2 Moulinè DMC floss in each of the following colors:

415	medium pearl gray
666	bright red
906	lime green
910	bright emerald green

- 1 Moulinè DMC floss in each of the following colors:

310	black
758	light terra cotta

- 1 white plastic ring with an internal diameter of 2 inches

- 1 spool of DMC Filomax in white

Border with little bird

- cotton Aida borders in white, finished with a red-scalloped edging (distributed by DMC). Width: 2 inches. Length: as needed

- 2 Moulinè DMC floss in each of the following colors:

647	dark gray
666	bright red
703	light grass green
783	gold
909	dark emerald green

- 1 Moulinè DMC floss in each of the following colors:

310	black
433	cacao
825	dark sky blue

- 1 white plastic ring with an internal diameter of 2 inches

- 1 spool of DMC Filomax in white

Directions

- Cut the strip in two and embroider the chosen motif on each of the two parts, starting and stopping at approx. 4 inches from the edges. Vertically center the motif and repeat until the desired length has been reached.

Finishings

- At the end, fold each strip in half, insert into the plastic ring, and sew the ends with the Filomax thread. Make a small hem on the wrong side of the fabric.

■ *Graphs of the motifs are on page 90*

Let's work together

Tie backs for small curtains

You will need: approx. 20 inches of Aida border in white, finished with red-scalloped edging (distributed by DMC). Width: approx. 2 inches, cotton Moulinè floss in each of the colors indicated in the color chart next to the graph, one metal ring with an internal diameter of approx. 2 inches, one hook to attach to the wall, and one spool of DMC Filomax in white. With a basting stitch, mark the center of the border and work the embroidery only on the right half, vertically centering the motif. At the end, remove the basting and fold the border in half. After having run it through the metal ring, sew the edges with the white Filomax thread. Make a small hem on the wrong side. Fix the hook to the wall, insert the curtain into the tie back to display the embroidered part, and attach the ring onto the hook.

Christmas Decorations

Here are two delightful motifs to embroider on white linen to add a cheerful touch to the Christmas season. Two beautiful Grecian borders have also been added to this "small" embroidery.

Embroidering

Work the embroidery in cross-stitch using two strands of Mouliné floss, following the instructions laid out on the provided graph and color chart. Each cross-stitch should fill, width-wise and height-wise, one square of fabric.

WHAT YOU NEED

• linen cloth in white (distributed by DMC) with approx. 100 threads in 4 inches for each motif. Length: 14 x 14 inches.

• 1 Moulinè DMC floss in each of the following colors:

For the border with snowmen

310	black
553	lilac
701	grass green
721	peach
727	light honey
747	very light sky blue
775	medium sky blue
813	medium delft blue
826	royal blue
827	light royal blue
891	dark petunia
958	aqua green
3810	light peacock blue
3820	amber
3825	light peach

For the border with trees

300	dark brick
472	light apple green
563	light jade green
891	dark petunia
909	dark emerald green
921	light copper
975	golden brown
977	light pumpkin
995	china blue
996	turquoise
3830	dark pink-beige

Directions

• Vertically and horizontally center the motif on the fabric and work the embroidery in cross-stitch and backstitch following the graph and color chart for each border.

• At the end, fold back the fabric along the edges and make a 1-inch hem.

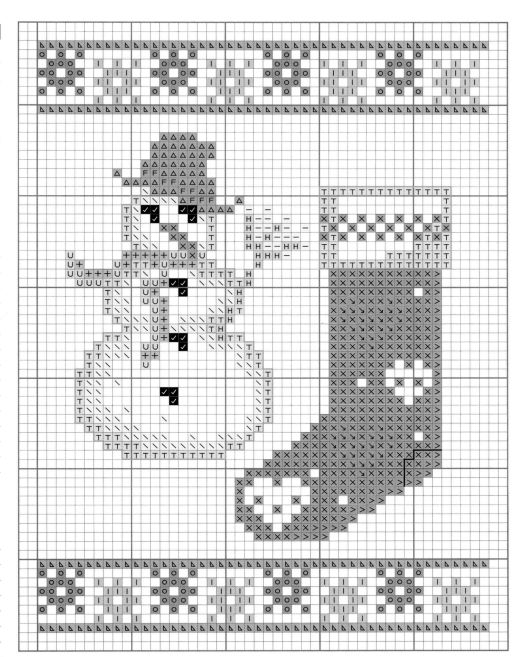

Above: graph of the snowmen motif to repeat at a regular distance from the other until the desired length has been reached.

							Backstitch:	
✓✓	310	⊾⊾	813	✗✗	891		—	310
>>	553	∘∘	826	ꜰꜰ	958		⁓	826
↘↘	701	❘❘	827	△△	3810			
++	721	＼＼	747	ʜʜ	3820			
−−	727	ᴛᴛ	775	ᴜᴜ	3825			

■ *Graph of the motif is on page 91*

55

Four Leaf Clovers and Spirals

Stylized four leaf clovers and a twisted cord pattern are embroidered in strong colors inspired by country braiding designs.

WHAT YOU NEED

For each border

• cotton Aida borders in white, finished with white edging (distributed by DMC). Width: 4 inches with approx. 64 squares in 4 inches. Length: as needed.

• 1 Mouliné DMC floss in each of the following colors:

For the border with spirals

208	dark lavender
340	medium blue violet
3689	light wine

For the border with four leaf clovers

311	dark blue
783	light mustard
900	dark orange
915	violet
3689	light wine
3746	light periwinkle

Directions

• Embroider in cross-stitch following the provided graph and color chart. Make sure that it is vertically centered and repeat the motifs until the desired length has been reached.

Embroidering

Work the embroidery in cross-stitch using two strands of Mouliné floss following the provided graph and color chart. Each cross-stitch should fill, width-wise and height-wise, one square of Aida canvas.

Graph of the two motifs that can be repeated until the desired length has been reached. For the border with the daisies, repeat the section indicated in the chart. Alternate each section between the yellow and orange diamonds.

208   340   3689

311   900   3689
783   915   3746

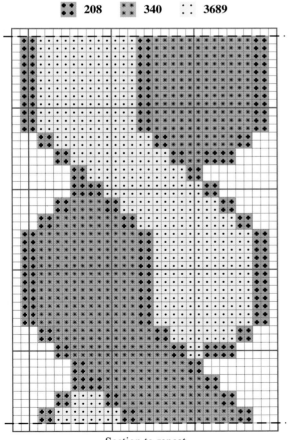

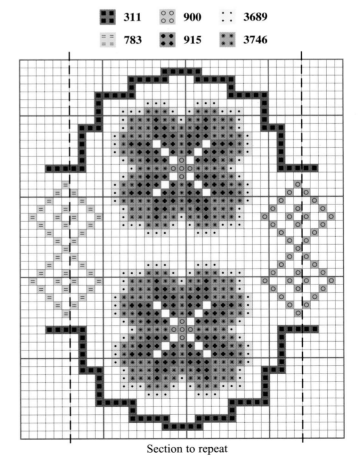

Section to repeat   Section to repeat

In the Pond

Ducks and frogs line up on a border that can be used to decorate baby clothes and linen.

For each border

• cotton Aida borders in white, finished with light blue or white edging (distributed by DMC). Width: 2 inches with approx. 60 squares in 4 inches. Length: as needed.

• 1 Moulinè DMC floss in each of the following colors:

For the border with ducks

310	black
321	dark red
517	dark aqua blue
677	wheat
725	dark honey
911	emerald green
924	dark silver green
954	light Nile green
3760	dark aqua blue
3818	brown green
3820	amber

For the border with frogs

310	black
368	light pistachio
469	dark yellow green
471	apple green
760	dark salmon
772	leaf green
819	light baby pink
972	dark gold yellow
3345	dark fern green

Directions

• Work the embroidery in cross-stitch following, for each border, the provided graph and color chart. Make sure that the motif is vertically centered and repeat it 3 inches from the other (for the frogs) and 2 inches (for the ducks) until the desired length has been reached. At the end, complete the embroidery by stitching the lines indicated on the graph in backstitch.

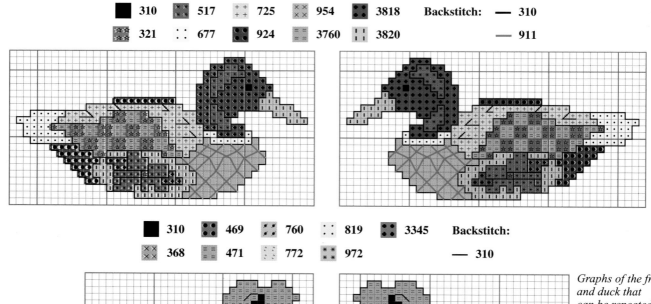

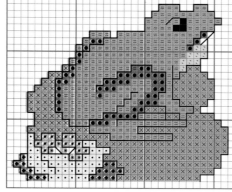
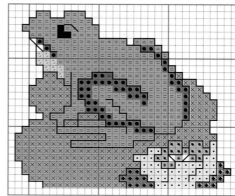

Graphs of the frog and duck that can be repeated until the desired length has been achieved. These motifs can also be in mirror mode (as shown) to create other ideas.

Embroidering

Work the embroidery in cross-stitch using two strands of Mouliné floss following the provided graph and color chart. Each cross-stitch should fill, width-wise and height-wise, one square of Aida canvas. For the backstitch, use one or two strands of Mouliné floss as indicated on the graph.

Little Red Berries

Little branches full of berries nestled between leaves and twigs create a horizontal motif that is both lively, delicate, and perfect for dressing up coordinated kitchen accessories.

Embroidering

Work the embroidery in cross-stitch using two strands of Moulinè floss following the provided graph and color chart. Each cross-stitch should fill, width-wise and height-wise, one square of Aida canvas.

For the small border

• cotton Aida borders in white, finished with light blue edging (distributed by DMC). Width: 4 inches with approx. 60 squares in 4 inches. Length: as required.

• 1 Moulinè DMC floss in each of the following colors:

310	black
321	dark red
470	yellow green
471	apple green
498	garnet
666	bright red
699	dark grass green
704	pale grass green
732	dark olive green
733	medium olive green
3348	light fern green

For the big border

• cotton Aida borders in white, finished with light blue edging (distributed by DMC). Width: 4 inches with approx. 60 squares in 4 inches. Length: as needed.

• 1 Moulinè DMC floss in each of the following colors:

310	black
321	dark red
470	yellow green
471	apple green
666	bright red
699	dark grass green
704	pale grass green
720	dark peach
722	medium peach
732	dark olive green
733	medium army green
972	dark gold yellow
3348	light fern green

Directions

• Work the embroidery in cross-stitch following, for each border, the provided graph and color chart. Make sure that the motif is vertically centered and repeat until the desired length has been reached.

■ *Graphs of the two borders are on pages 92 and 93*

Another Idea

A cheerful nosegay of colored flowers may substitute the berries to create a new motif using the magic color blend of the petals.

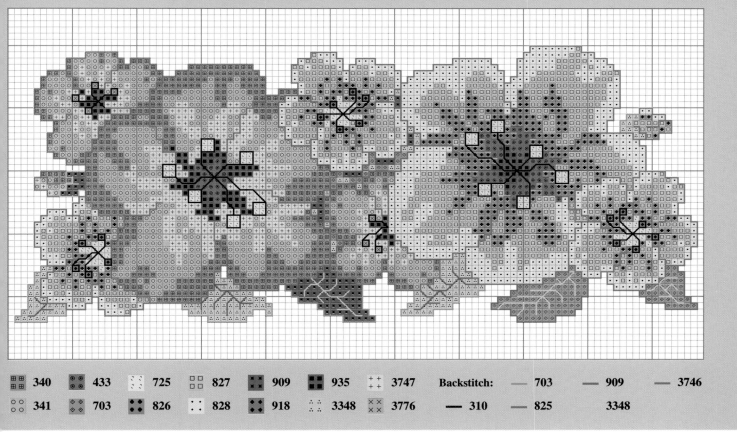

⊞⊞ 340	⊙⊙ 433	725	▢▢ 827	◆◆ 909	■■ 935	++ 3747
○○ 341	⊙⊙ 703	826	∴ 828	◆◆ 918	3348	×× 3776

Backstitch: — 703   — 909   — 3746   — 310   — 825   3348

Gathering in the Woods

It is possible to gather many things in the wood such as sweet, perfumed strawberries and delicious mushrooms. These are motifs that can give a cheerful touch to kitchen accessories.

WHAT YOU NEED

For the border with strawberries

• cotton Aida borders in white, finished with white edging (distributed by DMC). Width: 2 inches with approx. 60 squares in 4 inches. Length: as needed.

• 1 Moulinè DMC floss in each of the following colors:

	white
	white
304	dark red
310	black
312	medium blue
334	dark sky blue
666	bright red
743	dark yellow
906	lime green

For the border with mushrooms

• cotton Aida borders in white, finished with yellow edging (distributed by DMC). Width: 4 inches with approx. 60 squares in 4 inches. Length: as needed.

• 1 Moulinè DMC floss in each of the following colors:

310	black
321	dark red
420	golden brown
422	light golden brown
561	dark jade green
606	red orange
740	dark tangerine
742	sun yellow
743	dark yellow
761	salmon
801	light brown
813	medium sky blue
899	pale azalea pink
902	dark wine
909	dark emerald green
3829	dark ochre

Directions

• Work the embroidery in cross-stitch following, for each border, the provided graph and color chart. Make sure that the motif is vertically centered and repeat until the desired length has been achieved. At the end, complete the embroidery by stitching the lines indicated on the graph in backstitch.

■ *Graph of the strawberries is on page 91*

Embroidering

Work the embroidery in cross-stitch using two strands of Moulinè floss following the provided graph and color chart. Each cross-stitch should fill, width-wise and height-wise, one square of Aida canvas.

	321		561		742		813		3829	Backstitch:		
	420		606		743		899			— 310		— 801
	422		740		761		909			— 321		— 902

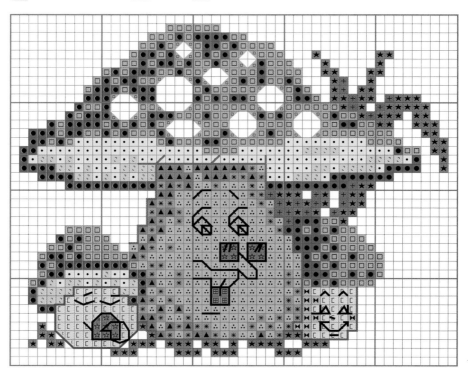

On the Beach

These colorful motifs give a cheerful and unusual touch to beach accessories.
These borders of differing widths can be put to any use.

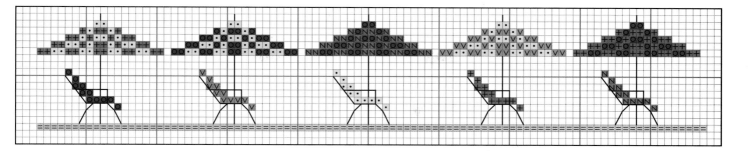

WHAT YOU NEED

- cotton Aida borders in white, finished with red, yellow, and turquoise edging (distributed by DMC). Width: one of 2 inches, one of 3 inches, and one of 4 inches. Length: as needed.

- 1 Mouliné DMC floss in each of the following colors:

310	black
317	light steel gray
318	pearl gray
606	red orange
703	light grass green
743	dark yellow
973	yellow gold
995	china blue
996	turquoise
3712	geranium

Directions

- Embroider in cross-stitch following, for each border, the provided graph and color chart. Position the bungalows on the 2-inch border, the slanted-closed umbrellas on the 3-inch border, and the umbrellas on the 4-inch border. Repeat until the desired length has been reached. At the end, complete the embroidery by stitching the lines indicated on the graph in backstitch.

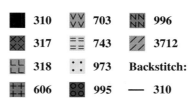

■ 310	ⱽⱽ 703	𝓝𝓝 996			
⊠ 317	☰ 743	⫽ 3712			
⊔ 318	⁚ 973	**Backstitch:**			
⊞ 606	◔◔ 995	— 310			

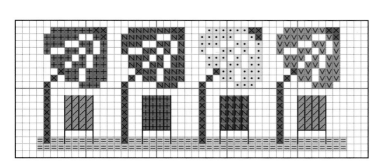

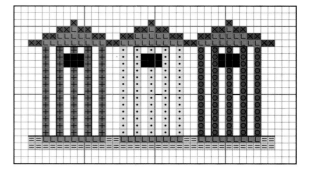

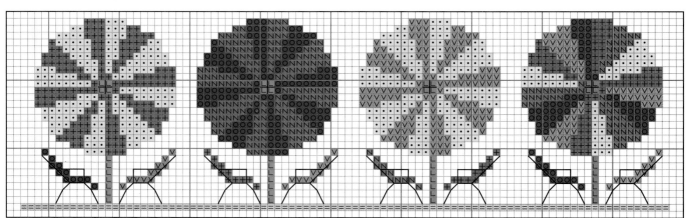

A Little Dress

The latest style for a nightgown is in cheerful red and white gingham. Romantic floral embroidery embellishes the two shoulder bands.

- cotton Aida borders in white, finished with a red bow edging (distributed by DMC). Width: 4 inches. Length: 40 inches.

- 1 Mouliné DMC floss in each of the following colors:

304	dark red
666	bright red
726	honey
727	light honey
3346	fern green
3347	medium fern green

- 1 nightgown in red and white gingham with shoulder bands of approx. 4 inches.

- 1 spool of DMC Filomax cotton in white.

Directions

- Cut the Aida border into two equal parts. On one part, work the embroidery in cross-stitch following the provided graph and color chart. Repeat the motif 4 times at a regular distance from the other. On the other strip of border, work the same embroidery but mirrored, in respect, to the other design.

Finishing

- Cut both the edges of the embroidered borders into a point and turn back a hem of approx. ½ an inch. Sew the borders onto the shoulder band by machine using the Filomax thread.

■ *Graphs of the motifs are on page 94*

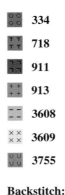

Embroidering

Work the embroidery in cross-stitch using two strands of Mouliné floss following the provided graph and color chart. Each cross-stitch should fill, width-wise and height-wise, one square of Aida canvas.

○ ○	334
T T	718
⊓	911
+ +	913
- -	3608
× ×	3609
U U	3755

Backstitch:

—	311
—	718

66

Another Idea

*Two motifs dedicated to your lingerie.
One motif can be embroidered, for example,
on to the pockets of a dressing gown.
The other can be embroidered
on a border for a nightgown;
both have a ribbon and flower theme.*

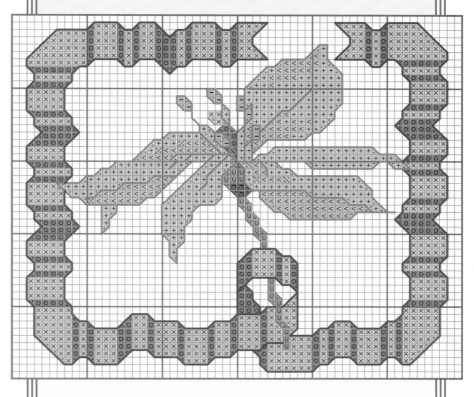

						Backstitch:
××	472	∪∪	783	++	973	
--	742	∞	906			— 904
⅂⅂	780	<<	972			— 946

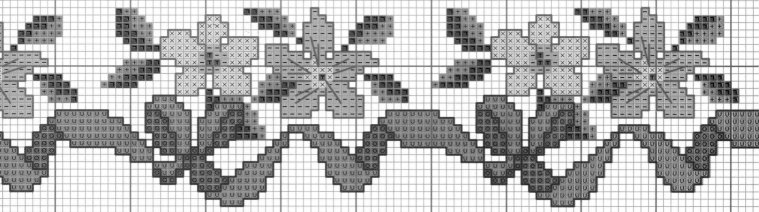

Summer

Sun, sand, sea and lots of little motifs to embroider on baby accessories.

WHAT YOU NEED

- 9 x 6 inches of Aida DMC cloth with approx. 55 squares in 4 inches (distributed by DMC) in white.

- 1 Moulinè DMC floss in each of the following colors:

310	black
436	an
553	lilac
601	dark fuchsia
602	fuchsia
604	medium pink

Directions

- Work the embroidery in cross-stitch centering the motif onto the fabric. These can be arranged as indicated in the photograph on this page. Alternate rows of boats, teddy bears, and butterflies, or the motifs can be used to create new compositions.

- At the end, after having starched and ironed the fabric on the reverse side, insert the fabric in a small frame or have it professionally framed.

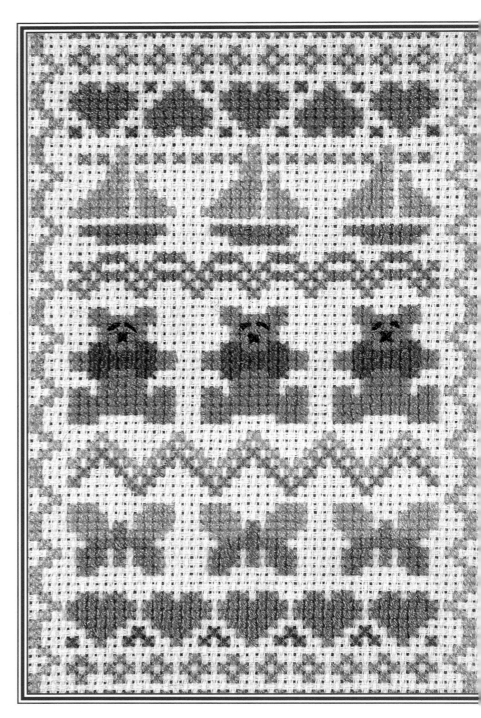

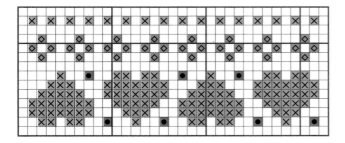

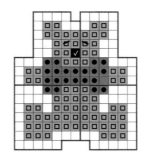

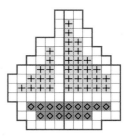

68

Embroidering

Work the embroidery in cross-stitch using two strands of Mouliné floss following the provided graph and color chart. Each cross-stitch should fill, width-wise and height-wise, one square of Aida canvas

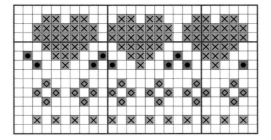

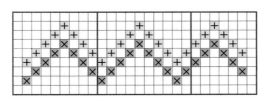

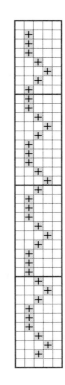

✓✓	**310**
▢▢	**436**
◇◇	**553**
●●	**601**
✕✕	**602**
++	**604**

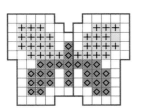

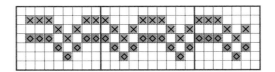

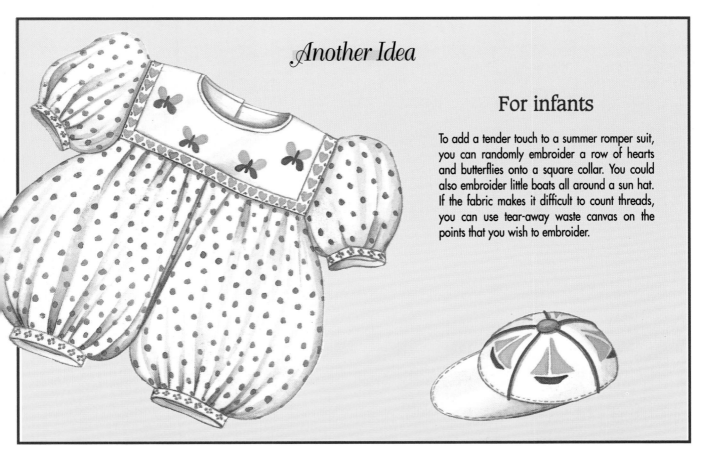

Another Idea

For infants

To add a tender touch to a summer romper suit, you can randomly embroider a row of hearts and butterflies onto a square collar. You could also embroider little boats all around a sun hat. If the fabric makes it difficult to count threads, you can use tear-away waste canvas on the points that you wish to embroider.

Having Fun

There are little motifs to embroider that are super easy. These motifs can be repeated as much as you desire. The cakes and the gift-wrapped boxes can also be embroidered separately. If you want bigger dimensions, all you have to do is work them on Aida canvas with 44 squares!

• 9 x 6 inches of Aida DMC canvas with approx. 55 squares in 4 inches (distributed by DMC) in white.

• 1 Mouline DMC floss in each of the following colors:

349	dark coral
605	pale fuchsia
700	dark grass green
702	medium grass green
725	medium gold
829	dark old brass
907	light lime green

Directions

• Work the embroidery in cross-stitch centering the motif on to the fabric. These can be arranged as indicated in the photograph on this page. Embroider little borders by alternating between rows of cakes and gift-wrapped boxes. The motifs could also be embroidered into new compositions. At the end, after having starched and ironed the fabric on the reverse side, insert the fabric in a small frame or have it professionally framed.

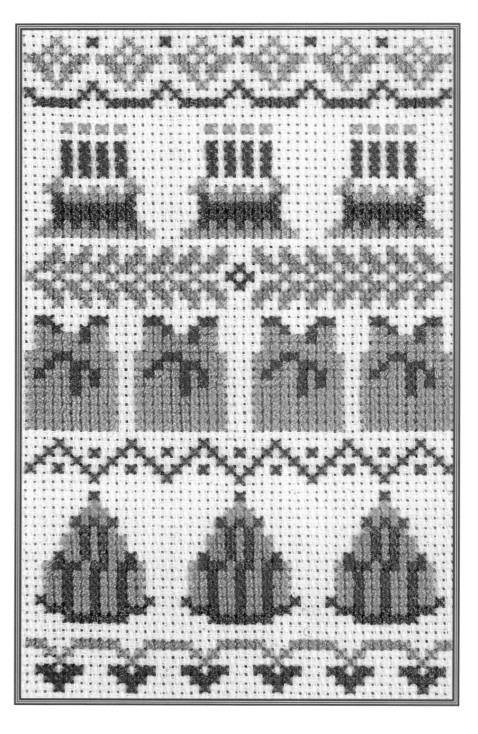

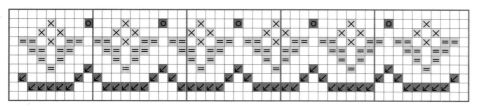

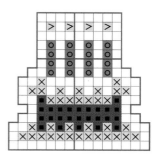

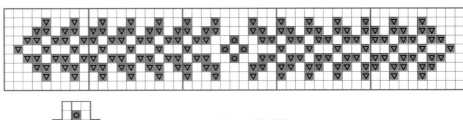

Embroidering

Work the embroidery in cross-stitch using two strands of Moulinè floss following the provided graph and color chart. Each cross-stitch should fill, width-wise and height-wise, one square of Aida canvas.

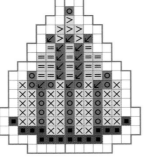

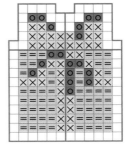

● ●	349	＞ ＞	725
✕ ✕	605	■ ■	829
◤ ◤	700	= =	907
▽ ▽	702		

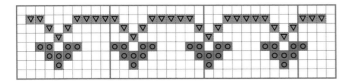

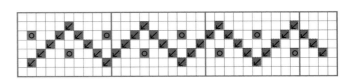

Another Idea

Ribbons to tie parcels and tags

The ribbons are little embroidered borders in Aida canvas, width of 1-inch (distributed by DMC). Use the provided graph and color chart and repeat until the desired length has been achieved. For the tags, it is better to embroider one of the smaller motifs.

Small and Refreshing embroidery

These borders are dedicated to children: houses, blooming balconies immersed in greenery, a delightful corner of a pond, and an irresistible parade of ducklings. This delightful motif is perfect for the creation of a sampler by simply adding a small alphabet chosen from the examples.

Embroidering

Work the embroidery in cross-stitch using two strands of Moulinè floss following the provided graph and color chart. Each cross-stitch should fill, width-wise and height-wise, one square of Aida canvas. For the backstitch, only one strand of Moulinè floss is required. Use two strands of Moulinè for the French knots.

- cotton Aida borders in white, finished with a yellow bow edging with approx. 60 squares in 4 inches (distributed by DMC). Width: 2 inches. Length: as needed.

- 1 Moulinè DMC floss in each of the following colors:

307	dark lemon yellow
310	black
700	dark grass green
703	light grass green
741	dark sun yellow
762	light pearl gray
826	sky blue
3078	light lemon yellow
3354	light antique rose

For the border with little girls

- cotton Aida borders in white, finished with a yellow bow motif with approx. 60 squares in 4 inches (distributed by DMC). Width: 4 inches. Length: as needed.

- 1 Moulinè DMC floss in each of the following colors:

211	lavender
301	brick
310	black
320	medium pistachio
400	dark brick
472	light apple green
553	light violet
646	light slate
727	very light gold
819	light baby pink
825	dark royal blue
910	bright emerald green
3354	light antique rose
3731	antique rose
3761	light aqua blue
3826	light golden brown

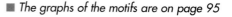

■ *The graphs of the motifs are on page 95*

72

For the motif with the houses

- 18 x 14 inches of regular woven linen canvas with approx. 110 threads in 4 inches (distributed by DMC) in white.

- 1 Moulinè DMC floss in each of the following colors:

310	black
702	medium grass green
704	pale grass green
725	medium gold
729	dark old gold
744	yellow
747	very light sky blue
754	peach
826	royal blue
904	dark lime green
907	light lime green
921	light copper
975	dark pumpkin
976	medium pumpkin
3801	red

Directions

- Work the embroidery with the houses centering the motifs on the linen canvas. Embroider the two motifs on the Aida borders making sure to vertically center them. Repeat each motif at a regular distance from the other for the entire length of the border.

- Complete the work by stitching the lines indicated on the graph in backstitch and French knots.

310	747	976
702	754	3801
704	826	
725	904	Backstitch:
729	907	— 904
744	921	— 975

THE FRENCH KNOT

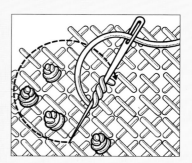

Bring the threaded needle to the right side of the fabric without pulling the needle through. Wind the thread around the needle 3 or 4 times and draw the needle through the knot. Stitch back into the fabric near the starting point, pulling the knot tight.

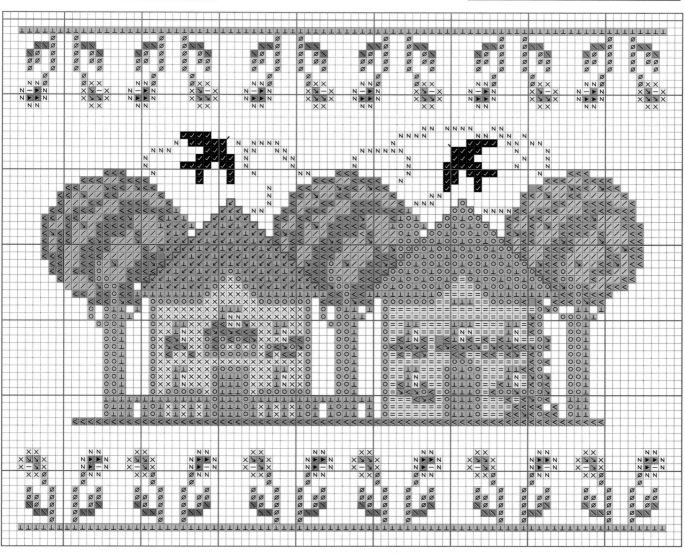

The Season of Flowers

Graphs of the two border motifs to repeat until the desired length has been reached.
The section that is to be repeated is in-between the dotted lines.

Border with yellow daisies

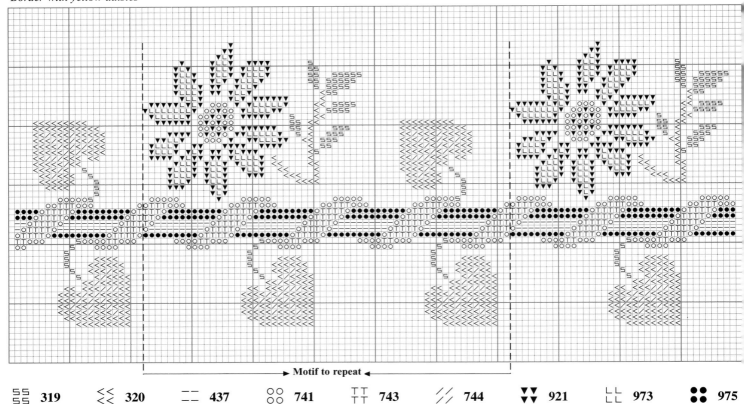

→ Motif to repeat ←

§§§§	**319**	<<<	**320**	−−	**437**	○○	**741**	TT TT	**743**	//	**744**	▼▼	**921**	LL LL	**973**

●● ●● **975**

Border with orange dahlias

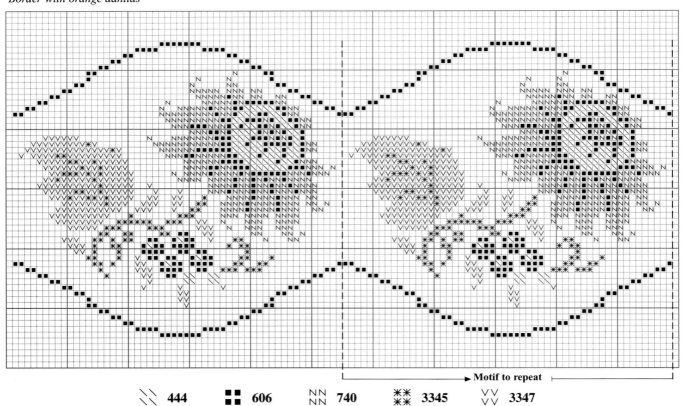

→ Motif to repeat ←

\\	**444**	■■ ■■	**606**	NN NN	**740**	✳✳ ✳✳	**3345**	VV VV	**3347**

A World of Little "Things"

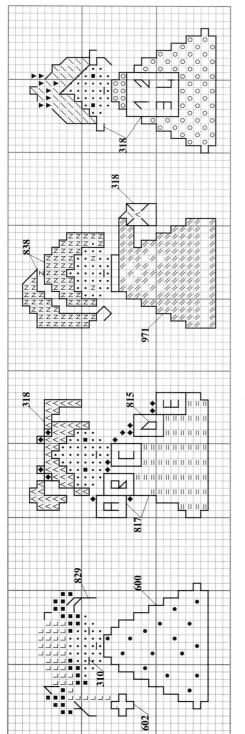

Graph of the border motif to repeat.

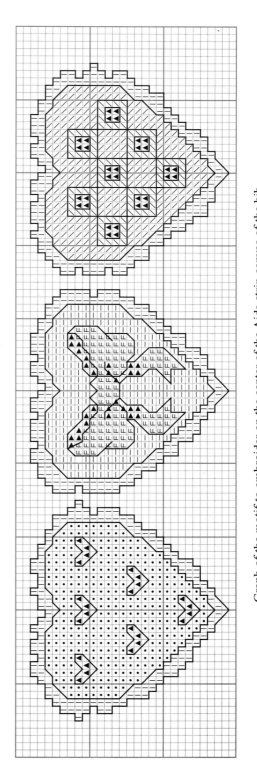

Graph of the motif to embroider on the center of the Aida strip canvas of the bib.

75

Mealtime and Bedtime

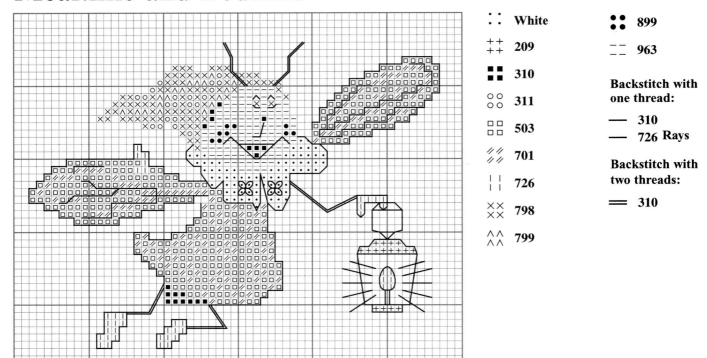

: :	White	:• :•	899
+ +	209	– –	963
■ ■	310		
○ ○	311		
□ □	503		
╱╱	701		
| |	726		
✕ ✕	798		
∧ ∧	799		

Backstitch with one thread:

— 310

— 726 Rays

Backstitch with two threads:

═ 310

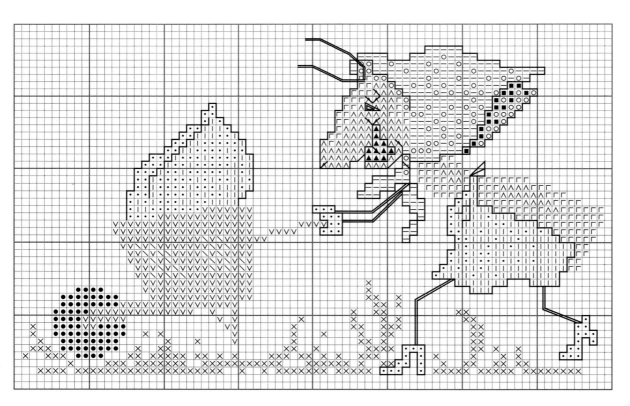

■ ■	347	⌐⌐	367	╲╲	422	✕✕	701	: :	743	– – 818
▲ ▲	349	∨∨	420	∧∧	503	||	742	○○	776	:• :• 869

Backstitch with one thread:

— 310

Backstitch with two threads:

═ 310

76

Dedicated to Infants

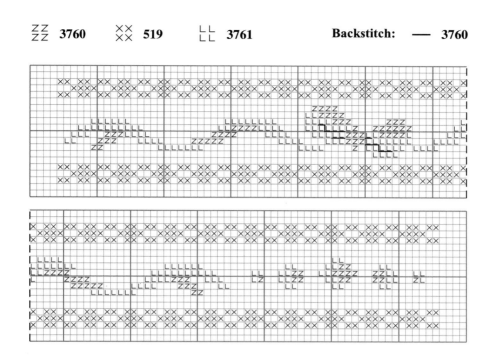

New Embroidery Ideas Bloom

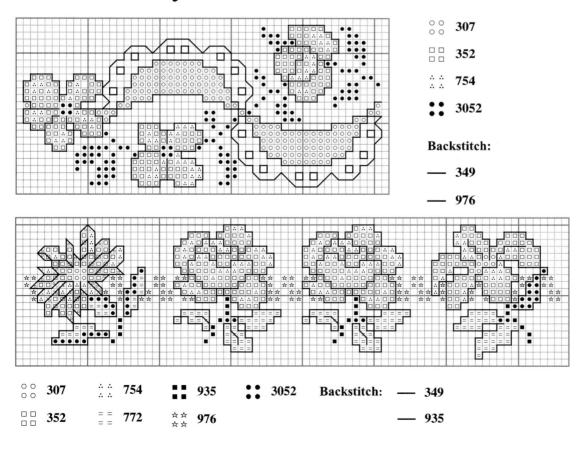

Miniature Ideas

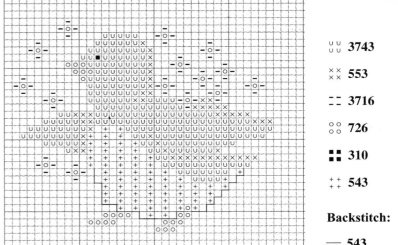

ᵁᵁ 3743

×× 553

⁻⁻ 3716

°° 726

■■ 310

⁺⁺ 543

Backstitch:

— 543

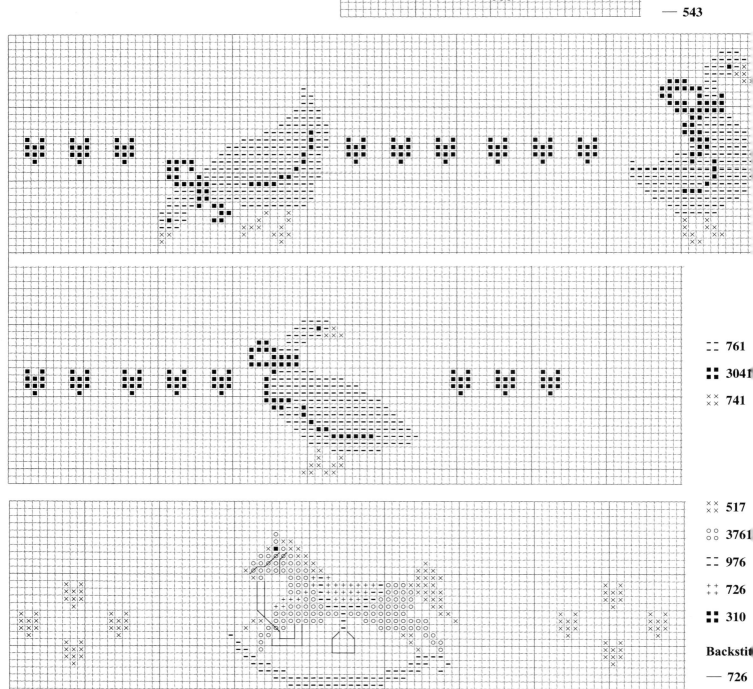

⁻⁻ 761

■■ 3041

×× 741

×× 517

°° 3761

⁻⁻ 976

⁺⁺ 726

■■ 310

Backstit⟨

— 726

Daisies and Love Knots

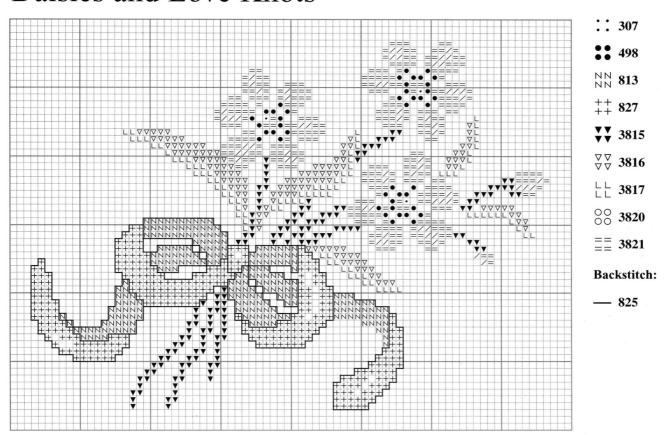

: : 307

●● 498

NN 813
NN

++ 827
++

▼▼ 3815

▽ ▽ 3816
▽ ▽

L L 3817
L L

○○ 3820

== 3821

Backstitch:

— 825

: : 307

●● 498

∕∕ 727

NN 813
NN

++ 827
++

▼▼ 3815

▽ ▽ 3816
▽ ▽

L L 3817
L L

== 3821

Backstitch:

— 825

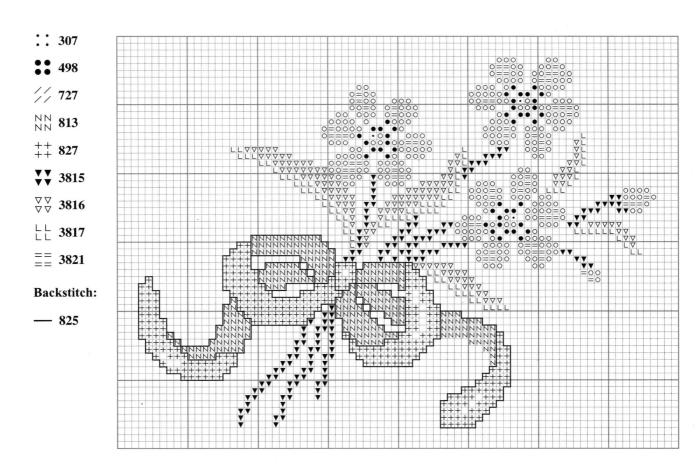

Little Roses and Moonflowers

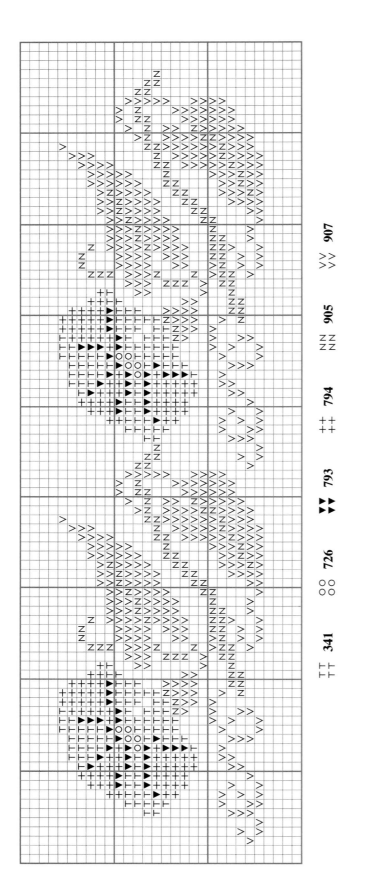

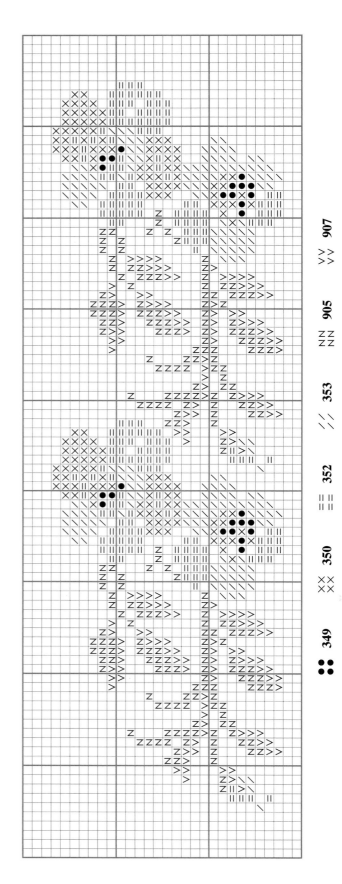

On Yellow and Blue Towels

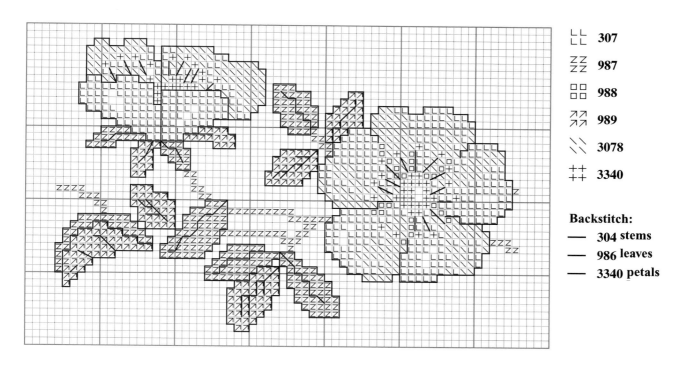

⌐⌐	**307**
ZZ	**987**
□□	**988**
↗↗	**989**
＼＼	**3078**
++	**3340**

Backstitch:
— **304** stems
— **986** leaves
— **3340** petals

Four Borders, Four Ideas

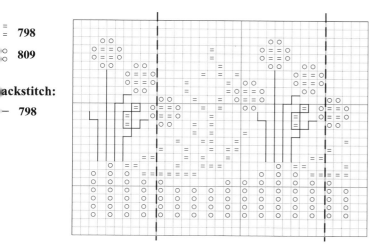

= **798**
∘ **809**

Backstitch:
— **798**

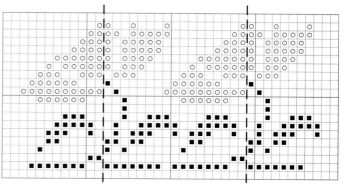

Repeat the motifs indicated in-between the dotted lines.

∘∘ **3801**   ■■ **3818**

Delicate Blooms

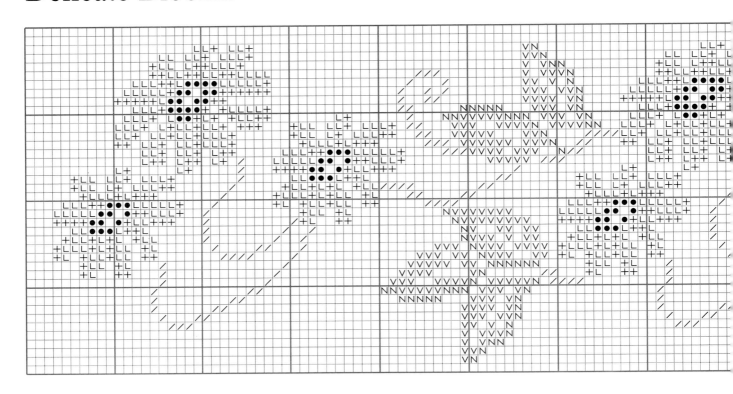

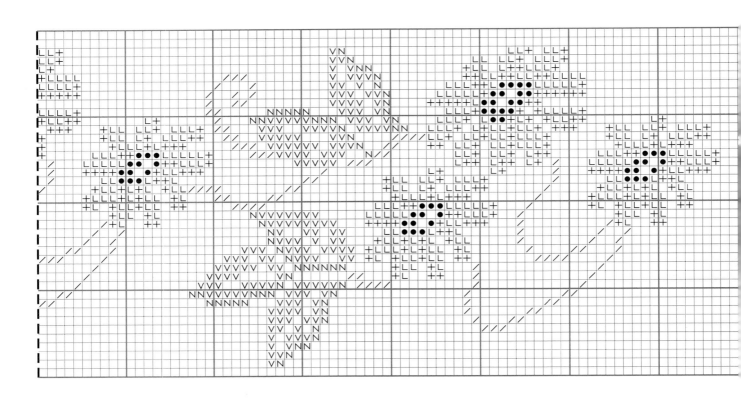

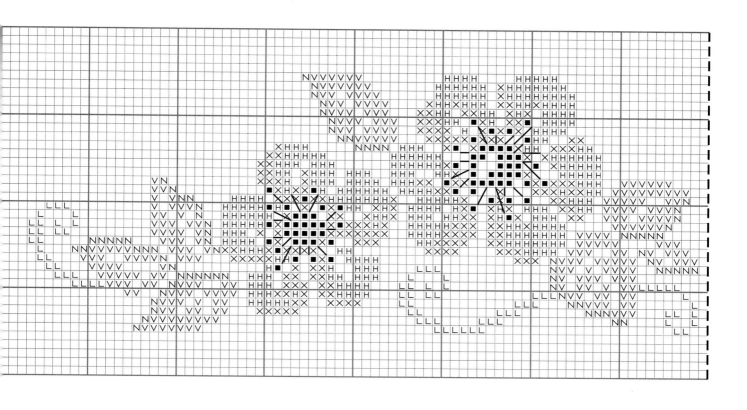

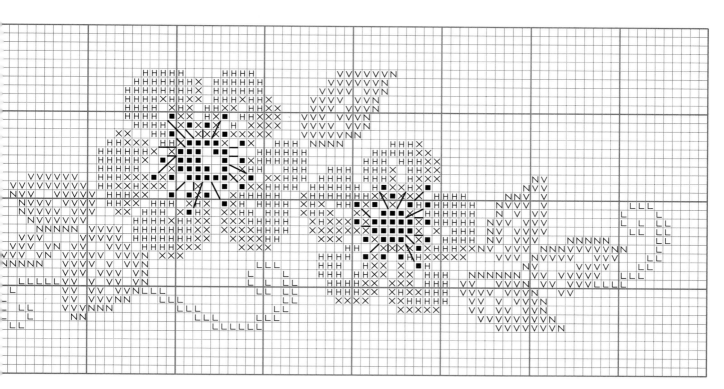

Perfume of Violets

To work the entire motif, join the charts printed on pages 84 and 85 along the dotted lines, overlapping the identical letters (A over A, B over B etc.). The dotted diagonal lines indicate the point at which the border will be folded to form the corner (the part of the border that remains empty corresponds to the part that will be folded under).

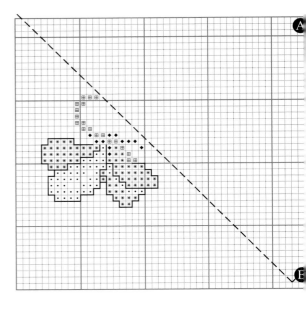

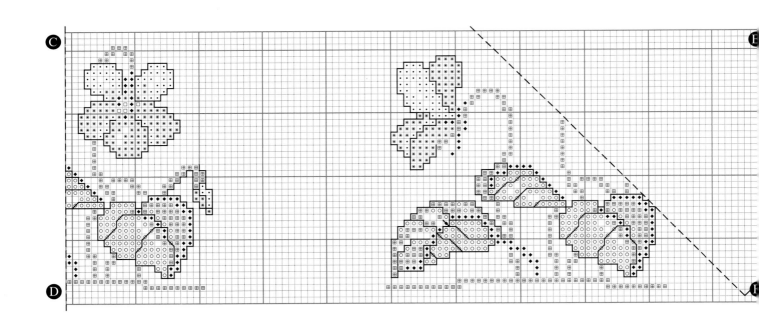

84

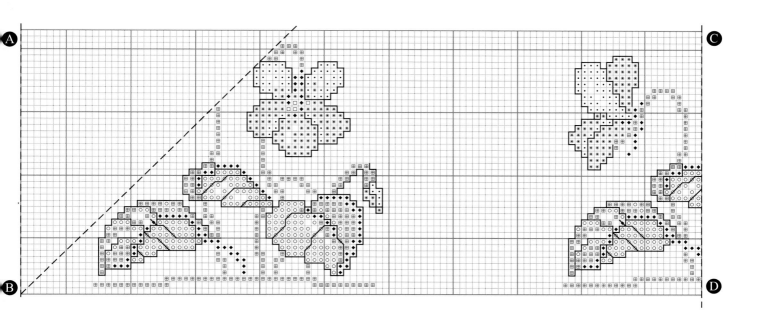

* * * *	208	□ □ □ □	743	✦ ✦ ✦ ✦	3345	○ ○ ○ ○	3348
∶ ∶	209	✚ ✚ ✚ ✚	745	⊞ ⊞ ⊞ ⊞	3347		

Backstitch:
—— 327 petals
—— 3345 leaves

Juniper Berries

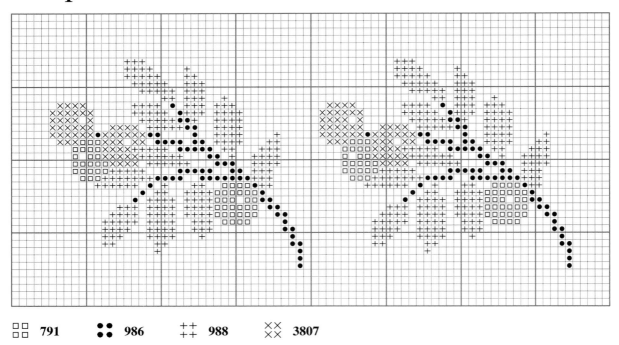

▢▢	791	●●	986	++	988	✕✕	3807

A Flower Meadow

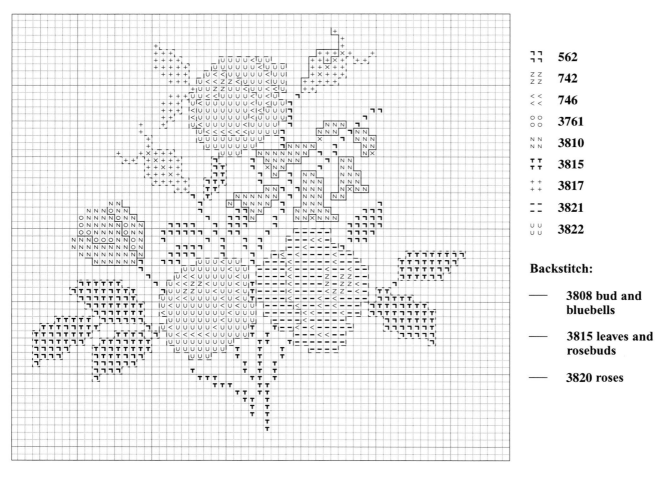

˥˥	562
ᶻᶻ	742
<<	746
ₒₒ	3761
ɴɴ	3810
⊤⊤	3815
++	3817
⁻⁻	3821
∪∪	3822

Backstitch:

—   **3808 bud and bluebells**

—   **3815 leaves and rosebuds**

—   **3820 roses**

Little Houses

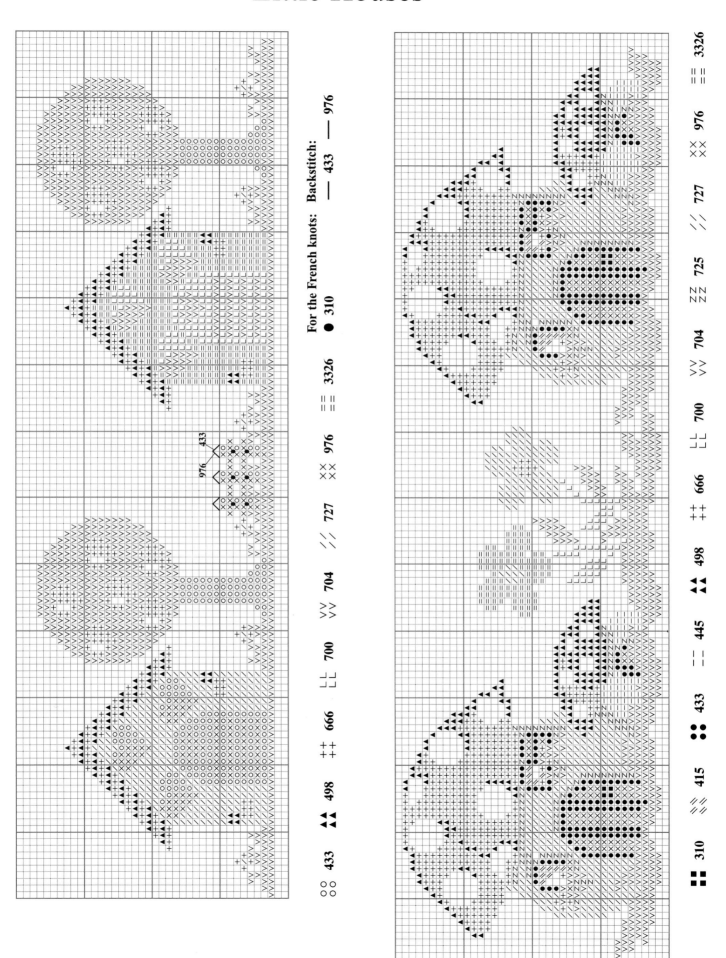

For the Kitchen

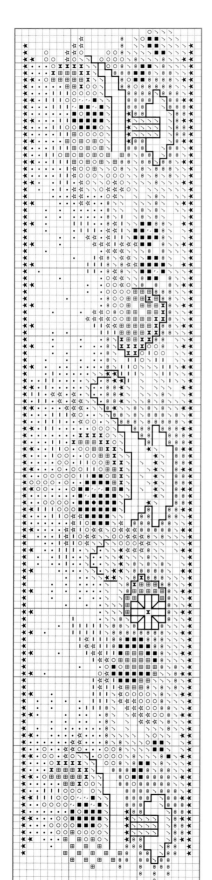

Backstitch in Mouliné:

— **414** vase on the left

— **300** lemon and pear

— **3363** inside of the lemon

— **3799** central vase and vase on the right

For the cross-stitch in Perlè:

★★ ★★	**317**	−− −−	**472**	✗✗ ✗✗	**745**
⊗⊗ ⊗⊗	**318**	■■ ■■	**666**	⁒⁒ ⁒⁒	**3326**
☆☆ ☆☆	**471**	⁞⁞ ⁞⁞	**743**	⊞⊞ ⊞⊞	**762**
				⚹⚹	**783**

For the cross-stitch in Mouliné:

∘∘ ∘∘	**3363**	●● ●●	**3799**

⁎⁎ ⁎⁎	**321**	⁼⁼	**471**	⬚⬚ ⬚⬚	**744**
		■■ ■■	**815**	●● ●●	**898**
		⁞⁞	**3326**		

Red Fruits
and Blue Fruits

Repeat the parts indicated between the dotted lines until the
desired length has been achieved.

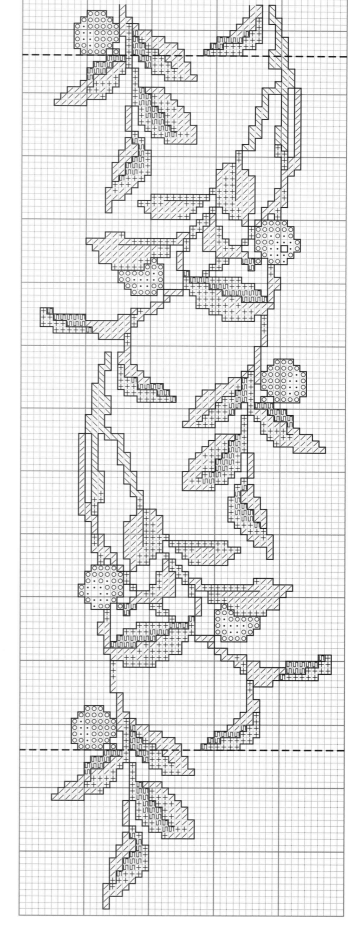

Backstitch:
— 796 blueberries
— 986 branches and leaves

/ /   472   : :   809   / /   907

○○   796   ++   905   ⊔⊔   986

89

Berries and Twigs

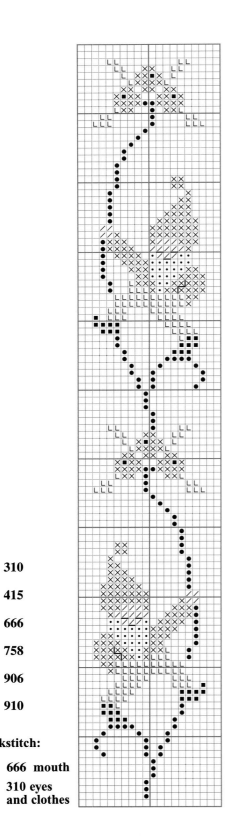

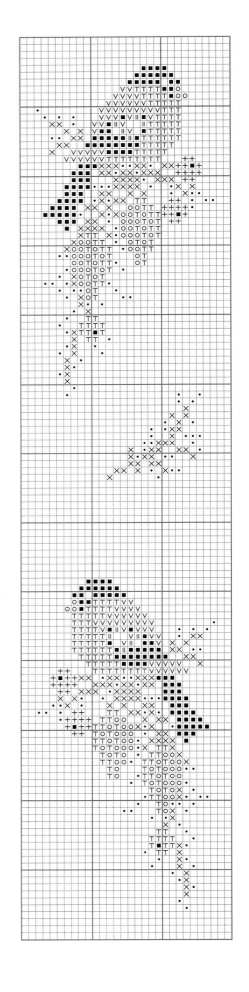

■■ 310
∷ 415
✕✕ 666
╱╱ 758
ʟʟ 906
●● 910

Backstitch:

— 666 mouth

— 310 eyes and clothes

■■ 310
ᴛᴛ 433
ᴠᴠ 647
++ 666
∷ 703
°° 783
‖‖ 825
✕✕ 909

Christmas Decorations

Graph of motifs to repeat on border at regular distances from each other.

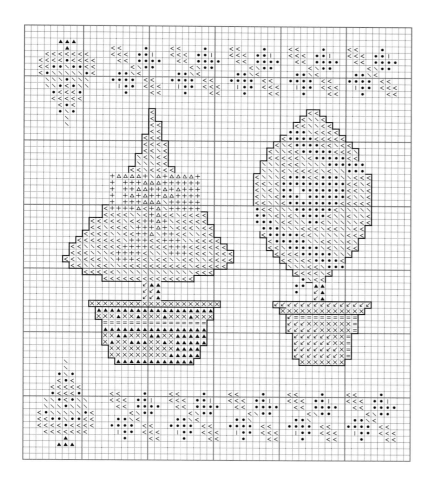

! !	472
\ \	563
• •	891
< <	909
× ×	921
▲ ▲	975
⌄ ⌄	977
△ △	995
+ +	996
= =	3830

Backstitch:
— 300 snowman
— 909 trees

Gathering in the Woods

Strawberry motif to repeat on the border until the desired length is reached.

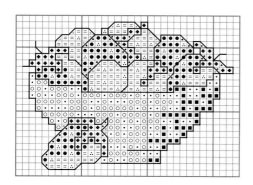

• •	white
• •	304
■ ■	312
○ ○	334
= =	666
∴ ∴	743
• •	906

Backstitch:
— 310

Little Red Berries (small border)

To work the entire motif, join the charts along the dotted lines overlapping the identical letters (A with A, B with B etc).

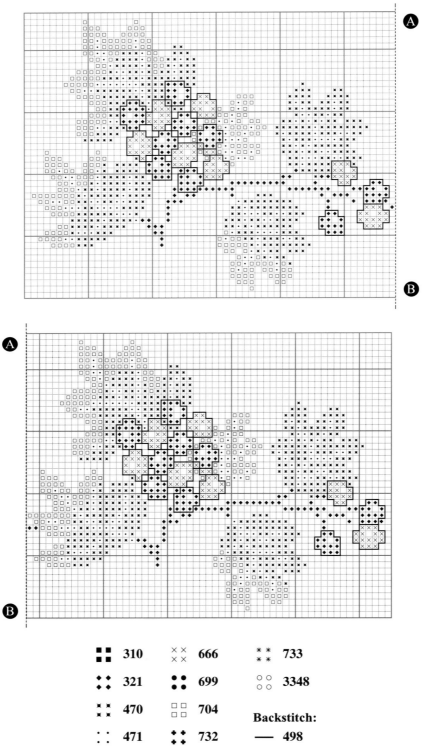

■■ 310	×× 666	** 733	
◆◆ 321	●● 699	○○ 3348	
×× 470	□□ 704		
∶∶ 471	✦✦ 732	**Backstitch:**	
		— 498	

Little Red Berries (large border)

To work the entire motif, join the charts along the dotted lines overlapping the identical letters (A with A, B with B etc).

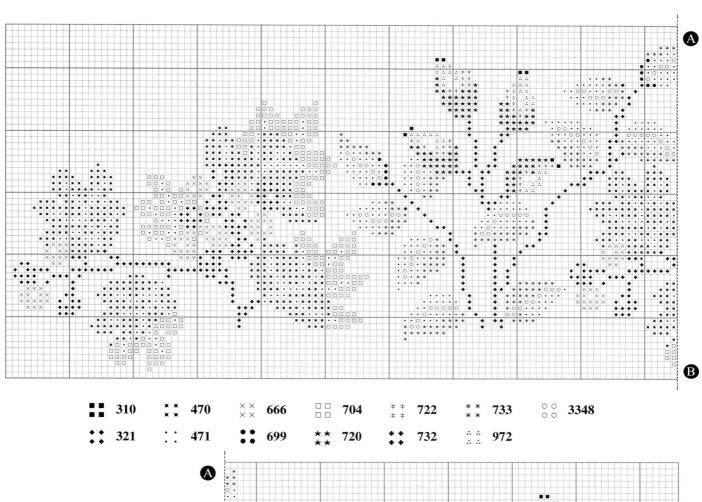

■■	310	✗✗	470	✗✗	666	□□	704	‡‡	722	✱✱	733	○○ 3348
◆◆	321	∴∴	471	●●	699	★★	720	◆‡	732	∴∴	972	

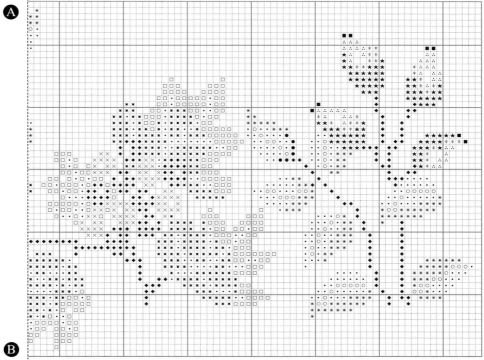

93

A Little Dress

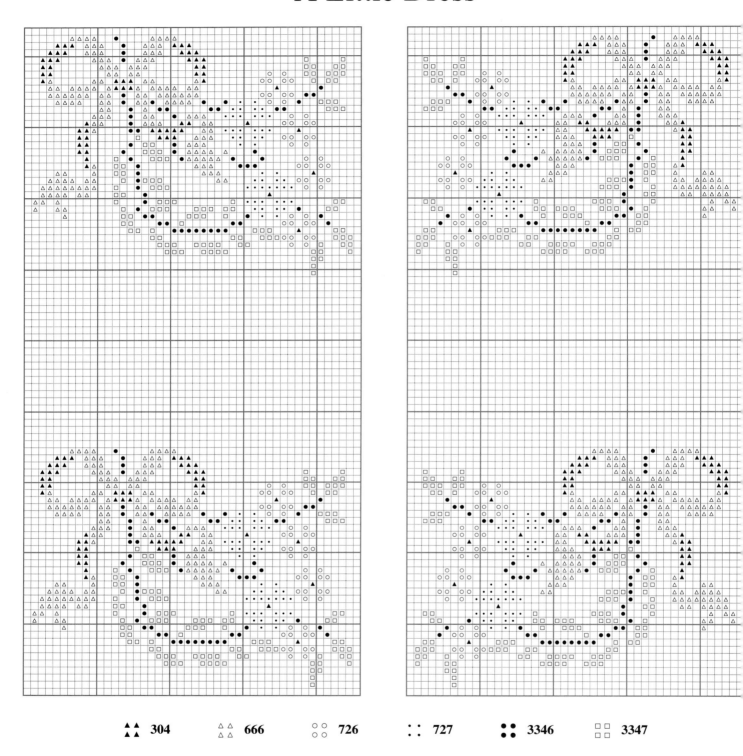

▲▲ 304	△△ 666	○○ 726	∶∶ 727	●● 3346	☐☐ 3347

Above: graph of the motifs to repeat, on the left and right shoulder bands, on the nightgown.

Small and Refreshing embroidery

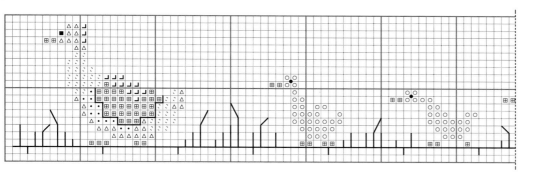

To obtain the entire border with the ducklings, join the graphs along the dotted lines.

○○ ○○	**307**	⊞⊞ ⊞⊞	**741**	∶∶	**3078**
■■ ■■	**310**	☆☆ ☆☆	**762**	⸴⸴	**3354**
△△ △△	**703**	⌐⌐ ⌐⌐	**826**		

Backstitch:

— 310 duckling wing

— 700 grass

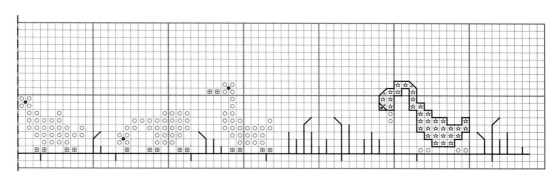

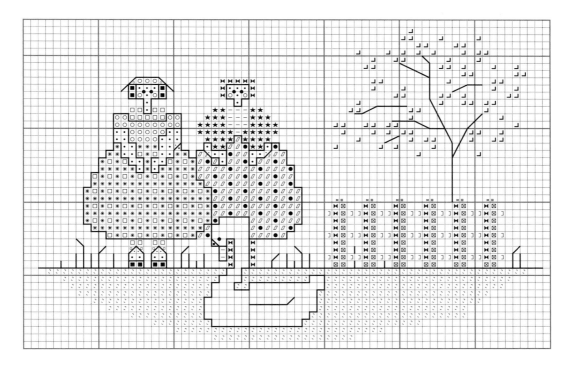

// //	**211**	⌐⌐ ⌐⌐	**320**	●● ●●	**553**	★★ ★★	**825**	⸴⸴	**3761**
⋈⋈ ⋈⋈	**301**	⊠⊠ ⊠⊠	**400**	−− −−	**727**	○○ ○○	**3354**	⌐⌐	**3826**
■■ ■■	**310**	□□ □□	**472**	∶∶	**819**	**★** **★**	**3731**		

Backstitch:

— 400 branches of the tree

— 553 lilac dress

— 646 contours of the swan

— 910 grass

— 3354 legs and faces

— 3731 dress and pink hat

95

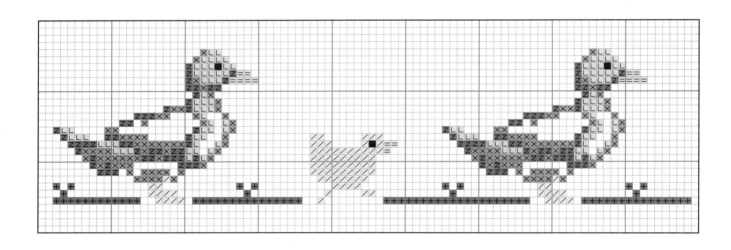